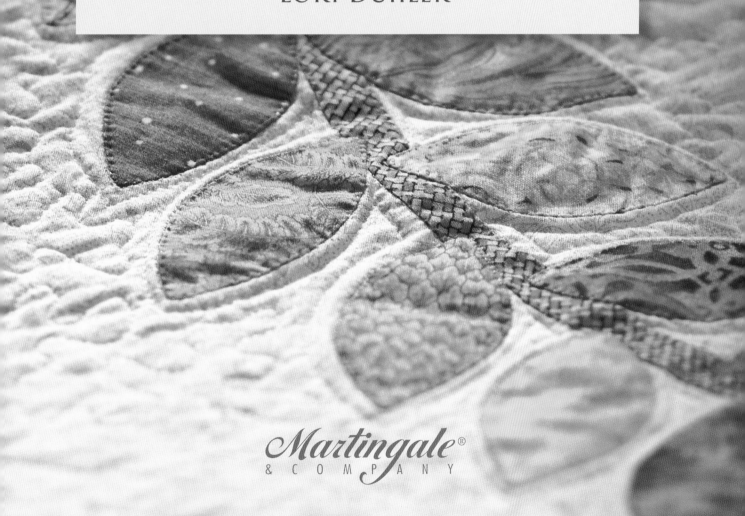

Quilter's Happy Hour

11 QUILTS WITH COCKTAIL RECIPES

LORI BUHLER

Martingale®
& COMPANY

Quilter's Happy Hour: 11 Quilts with Cocktail Recipes
© 2008 by Lori Buhler

Martingale®
& COMPANY

That Patchwork Place® is an imprint of
Martingale & Company®.

Martingale & Company
20205 144th Ave. NE
Woodinville, WA 98072-8478 USA
www.martingale-pub.com

Printed in China
13 12 11 10 09 08   8 7 6 5 4 3 2 1

Library of Congress
Cataloging-in-Publication Data
Library of Congress Control Number: 2007037795

ISBN: 978-1-56477-767-6

Credits

President & CEO ✦ *Tom Wierzbicki*
Publisher ✦ *Jane Hamada*
Editorial Director ✦ *Mary V. Green*
Managing Editor ✦ *Tina Cook*
Developmental Editor ✦ *Karen Costello Soltys*
Technical Editor ✦ *Laurie Baker*
Copy Editor ✦ *Melissa Bryan*
Design Director ✦ *Stan Green*
Illustrator ✦ *Adrienne Smitke*
Cover Designer ✦ *Stan Green*
Text Designer ✦ *Trina Craig*
Photographer ✦ *Brent Kane*

Cocktail recipes are from *Bartender's Black Book*,
published by the Wine Appreciation Guild, South San
Francisco, www.wineappreciation.com. Reprinted by
permission of the publisher.

Mission Statement

Dedicated to providing quality products and
service to inspire creativity.

Dedication

To my mother, Carolyn Branstner, who taught me to sew
and gave me an appreciation for all things handmade.

Acknowledgments

Special thanks to my quilting friends, the Cal-Co
Quilters' Guild and the Ladies of the Lake, who inspire
me with their talent and creativity. To Salinda Ashe,
who shared the interfacing technique with me many
years ago; and to Doris Kaiser, for letting me bounce
ideas off her and for taking me seriously when I told
her I wanted to do this project. And last but not least,
my love and thanks to my daughter, Amanda, who has
visited countless quilt shops against her will, and my
husband, Dave, who loves my quilts so much that he
shares them with the dog.

Contents

The Quilts

Introduction

I feel the hours I spend sewing should be "happy hours," not stressful, so for a long time I avoided appliqué patterns and patterns with curved pieces because I knew the anxiety they would bring. Then one day a fellow quilt-guild member introduced me to a technique that forever changed my outlook on those designs I'd been avoiding for so long. The technique involved using interfacing to face appliqué shapes. The facing made it possible to turn under the edges of the appliqué with perfect results!

Once I started doing appliqué using the interfacing technique, I began to think of other ways this method could be used, especially for the look of curved piecing. Wouldn't it be great if both of my areas of avoidance could be solved with one technique? I decided to experiment with a simple Drunkard's Path pattern. After many happy hours of sewing, I deemed the technique a success for curved piecing as well! All I needed to do was turn the curved shape into an appliqué. A vast world of possibilities was now available to me, and quilts that I had admired but was too intimidated to attempt were suddenly within my reach.

Some of you may already be familiar with the interfacing technique, but for those of you who aren't or for those who need a brief refresher, I've given step-by-step instructions beginning on page 5. Other techniques that I've used throughout the book are covered in "General Instructions," beginning on page 7. The remainder of the book is devoted to the 11 projects I designed using the interfacing technique. I was inspired to name my quilts after drinks when I purchased a piece of floral fabric that reminded me of a tropical sunrise. Because I had just returned from a vacation to Mexico, my next thought was that "Tequila Sunrise" would be a perfect name. Both quilts and cocktails have a tradition of bearing fanciful names, so naming the rest of the quilts was easy. As an added bonus, recipes are included for the drinks after which the quilts are named.

May all your quilting hours be happy hours!

~Lori

The Interfacing Technique

Any lightweight nonfusible interfacing can be used for this technique. However, I use a product called Pattern Ease from Handler Textile Corp., which is much like interfacing but is classified by the manufacturer as a pattern-tracing material. Like interfacing, it is lightweight and nonfusible, but what I really like about it is that it is 45" wide; most interfacings are only about 22" wide. All the yardage amounts and cutting instructions in this book assume you will be using a 45"-wide product. If you are unable to find Pattern Ease or a 45"-wide interfacing, double the interfacing yardage needed for each pattern.

1. Follow the project instructions to cut the interfacing into strips the width specified. You will also cut fabric strips of the same width.

2. Using a pen, trace the pattern provided with the project onto template plastic. Cut out the template.

3. Place the template on the interfacing strip and trace around the shape with the pencil. If your template has a straight edge, place that straight edge along the cut edge of the strip. Trace the amount of shapes needed, following the illustrations where given to make the best use of your interfacing strip. Leave approximately ½" of space between each shape.

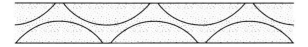

Note: The interfacing strips are often longer than the fabric strips, so check the lengths against each other to make sure you don't trace more than will fit onto the fabric strip when the strips are layered together.

4. Lay the interfacing strip, marked side up, on the right side of the fabric strip of the same width. Be sure that none of the traced shapes are in the selvage area of the fabric strip. Pin the strips together in the areas between the shapes.

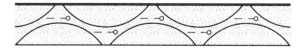

5. Sew on the marked lines, backstitching at the beginning and end of each seam.

6. Cut out each shape, leaving at least ⅛" for a seam allowance but no more than ¼". Turn each piece right side out. For shapes that have been completely stitched around, you will need to cut a slit in the interfacing only and then turn the shape to the right side. I use a turning tool called "That Purple Thang," from Little Foot Ltd., to help me push out the stitched edges completely. When turning, roll the fabric slightly to the interfacing side to prevent the interfacing from showing on the front of the quilt. Use an iron to press each shape from the fabric side.

7. Position the turned shape on the background fabric and machine appliqué it in place along the edges, using a blanket stitch or blind hem stitch. You can also use a narrow zigzag stitch, but I don't like it as well because it tends to flatten the edges of the shape and doesn't look as much like a hand stitch as the blanket stitch or blind hem stitch. This is purely a personal preference. Experiment with the stitches on your sewing machine to find the right stitch for you.

Blanket stitch

Blind hem stitch

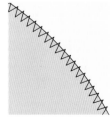

Narrow zigzag stitch

All my quilts are appliquéd using clear monofilament. You may prefer to use a thread that matches the appliqué piece, or even a contrasting thread if that is your preference. I find that using an open-toe foot is helpful for seeing as you sew. Although I machine appliqué my pieces, the interfacing technique may also be used for hand appliqué or the appliqué method of your choice.

8. If the appliqué piece will be part of a seam, such as on the edge of a block, I trim away the fabric and interfacing under the appliqué, leaving approximately a ¼" seam allowance. If the piece is not in a seam, trimming is a personal choice. It is not necessary if you will be machine quilting, but if you are quilting by hand, you may want to cut out the extra layers to reduce the bulk you will be quilting through.

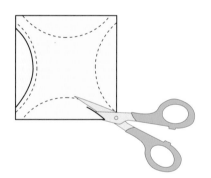

General Instructions

In this section you'll find instructions for specific techniques, including paper piecing and cutting bias strips, as well as information on the process I use for adding borders. The basics of finishing your quilts are also given here. If you are new to quilting, check with your local quilt shop for beginning quiltmaking classes, or invest in a good reference book, such as *Your First Quilt Book (or it should be!)* by Carol Doak (Martingale & Company, 1997).

BEFORE YOU BEGIN

Here are some points to keep in mind as you sew your projects.

- All yardages listed are based on 42"-wide fabric.
- A rotary cutter, mat, and clear acrylic ruler are needed for rotary cutting. A good pair of sharp scissors is required for cutting out appliqué shapes and trimming away excess fabric.
- Read all instructions thoroughly before beginning any project.
- Prewashing and pressing your fabrics is a personal choice. I rarely prewash my fabrics, but that is my own preference. When in doubt, prewash.
- Sew with the right sides of the fabric pieces together and use ¼" seam allowances, unless otherwise specified. Seam allowances are included in the cutting sizes listed, and an accurate ¼" seam allowance is very important for ensuring that the pieces fit together properly.

PAPER PIECING

For "Raspberry Kiss" (page 55) and "Blue Canary" (page 62), the appliqué shapes are paper pieced before they are applied to the interfacing. Paper piecing is a great way to achieve perfect points, as you can see in the photos of these two projects.

For added ease in handling the fabrics, I like to cut my fabric into strips rather than using chunks. The cutting instructions for these projects will indicate the proper width of the strips.

1. Photocopy the appliqué pattern provided with the project, reproducing it the number of times indicated in the instructions. Your local quilt shop probably carries paper specifically designed for paper piecing, but I find that the paper from the photocopier works just fine. Cut out each pattern slightly beyond the dashed outer line. The printed side of the pattern will be the side you stitch from; the unprinted side will be the side on which you place your fabrics. Solid lines indicate lines on which you will stitch. The dashed line around each pattern is the cutting line.

2. The sections are numbered and will be covered and stitched in order. With the printed side of the pattern facing up, lay a section 1 fabric strip under section 1, wrong side up, so that the end of the strip extends into section 2 by at least ¼". With the printed side of the

paper facing you, hold the pattern and fabric up to a light source to make sure the fabric covers section 1 entirely and extends past the section 1 lines by at least ¼" on all sides. Pin the fabric in place from the printed side of the pattern. Trim away the excess strip.

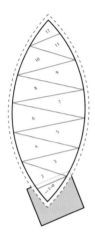

3. With right sides together, position the section 2 fabric strip so that it covers section 1 and the end of the strip extends at least ¼" past the sewing line between sections 1 and 2. Using a stitch length of 18 to 20 stitches per inch, sew on the line between sections 1 and 2, beginning and ending 2 to 3 stitches beyond the line.

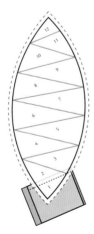

4. Flip the section 2 fabric into place to confirm that it covers the entire area. Trim the strip so that it is at least ¼" larger than section 2 on all sides, and then flip back the section 2

piece and trim the seam allowance between sections 1 and 2 to ¼". Press the section 2 fabric into place.

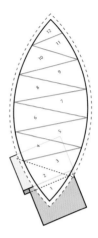

5. Continue adding pieces in numerical order until the foundation is completed. Trim the pattern along the dashed outer line. Do not remove the paper until the foundation is sewn to the interfacing according to the pattern instructions.

CUTTING BIAS STRIPS

Bias strips are needed for vine appliqués in several of the patterns.

1. Use a long acrylic ruler and your rotary cutter to square up the left edge of the fabric. Working with a single layer of fabric, place the 45° angle of your ruler along the lower-left edge of the fabric. Position the ruler so that it extends completely across the fabric. Cut along the edge of the ruler.

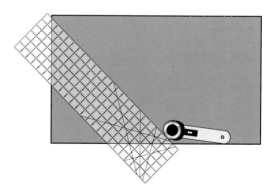

2. Measuring from the cut edge, cut strips of the desired width. You are cutting on the bias edge of the fabric, so handle the strips carefully to avoid stretching them.

Adding Borders

All the quilts in this book have borders with butted corners. Some of the quilts call for cutting strips along the lengthwise grain, and some involve cutting strips from selvage to selvage. Lengths listed in the cutting instructions for borders cut along the lengthwise grain are longer than needed so that you can measure your quilt top and cut them to the exact length. Some selvage-to-selvage strips may need to be pieced together to achieve the desired length. To do this, place the strips right sides together at a right angle and stitch from corner to corner. Trim the seam allowance to ¼", and press it open.

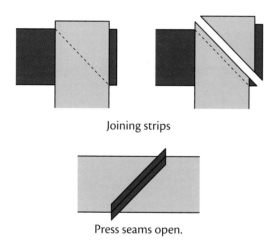

Joining strips

Press seams open.

Measure the length of your completed quilt top through the center of the quilt. Cut your side border strips to this measurement. Sew the borders to the sides of the quilt top, easing to fit if necessary. Measure across the width of the top, including the two border strips you just added. Cut the two remaining borders to this measurement and sew them to the top and bottom edges of the quilt. Repeat to add any remaining borders.

Finishing Techniques

Your quilt top may be finished, but there's still a bit more to be done. Follow the guidelines in this section to assemble the quilt sandwich, quilt the layers together, and add binding and a label.

Layering and Basting

1. Cut the backing and batting at least 1½" to 2" larger on all sides than the quilt top. For most projects, you will need to piece the backing fabric to achieve the necessary size.

2. Lay the backing wrong side up on the floor or a large, flat surface. Smooth it out and secure the edges with masking tape. The backing should be taut but not stretched. Place the batting over the backing. Lay the quilt top, right side up, on top of the batting. Working from the center outward, smooth out the top.

3. Baste the layers together. I use curved safety pins made especially for basting, but you may also thread baste. Place the safety pins no farther apart than a spread hand's width. To thread baste, take long running stitches from the center to each corner, and then create a grid pattern with stitching lines approximately 6" to 8" apart. Baste along the outside edges to finish.

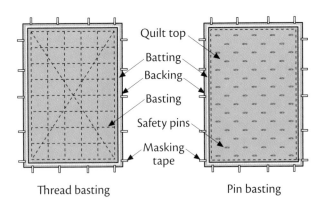

Quilt top
Batting
Backing
Basting
Safety pins
Masking tape

Thread basting   Pin basting

Machine Quilting

While I am by no means an expert on machine quilting, I have learned a few things over the years. When I first started machine quilting, I mainly quilted in the ditch or followed quilting patterns that I had marked on the top with a stencil. Unfortunately, I always ended up with bumps and puckers. At the time, I was using polyester batting, because that was what I had always used for hand quilting. Once I started using cotton batting, some of these problems were eliminated. Cotton makes the layers stick together and not slide as much.

I have found that marking a quilt top for quilting is one of my least favorite activities, so now almost all my quilting is free-motion and involves no marking. If you have never done this, you really should give it a try. If you can draw it, you can stitch it. You may want to practice on some scrap fabric and batting first. I use clear mono-filament, which doesn't show the inconsistencies in my stitching. I use a regular sewing machine, and although the bed on mine is a little bit larger than average, it is possible to quilt a large quilt with it.

In a quilting class I took a number of years ago, the instructor made a statement that really stuck with me. She said, "As you are pushing the heavy quilt through your machine and your shoulders are aching, just say over and over, 'It would take me six months to hand quilt this quilt, it would take me six months to hand quilt this quilt. . . .'"

With each quilt's instructions, I include suggestions for the quilting design. I am usually frustrated by patterns that read "quilt as desired," because I would like to have at least some idea of what to do. Although I give the details of how I quilted my projects, feel free to quilt yours in any way you please. Maybe my ideas will allow you to think in a different direction for your own quilting.

The following are some general guidelines for machine quilting:

- Basting is important. Make sure all your layers are flat and smooth and that you've used enough pins or thread to prevent the layers from shifting.

- One of the most common forms of straight-line quilting is called "in the ditch." It involves stitching just beside a seam line on the side without the seam allowance. In most cases, this technique requires a walking foot for your machine. This will help feed all the layers through your machine at the same rate.

- Use an open-toe foot and drop the feed dogs for free-motion quilting. This technique allows you to move the quilt in any direction. This is the method I prefer, but it does require practice.

- When you have your quilt in your machine, make sure the area on which you are working is flat and not bunched up. Try to keep the weight of the quilt from pulling at the sewing area, which makes it difficult to move the quilt smoothly as you stitch.

- Free-motion quilting uses a lot of thread, so be prepared. Wind several bobbins before you start so that you don't have to remove the quilt from the machine more often than necessary.

Binding

I use the overlapped-corners binding method, in which each side of the quilt is bound separately. The cutting instructions will indicate the number of 3"-wide straight-grain strips to cut.

1. Cut the backing and batting even with the edges of the quilt top.

2. Join the binding strips at right angles to make one long strip. Trim ¼" from the stitching and press the seam allowances open.

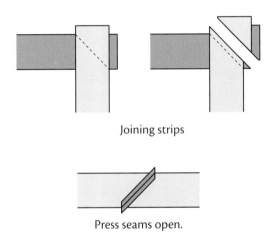

Joining strips

Press seams open.

3. Fold the binding strip in half lengthwise, wrong sides together, and press the entire length.

4. Measure the width of the quilt top and cut two binding strips slightly longer than this measurement. Pin the strips to the top and bottom edges of the quilt front, aligning the raw edges and leaving some excess extending beyond each end. Stitch the binding in place. I use a walking foot and lengthen my stitch length. Trim the ends of the binding strips even with the sides of the quilt.

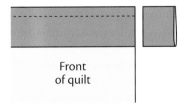

Front of quilt

5. Fold the binding to the back of the quilt and pin it in place.

Back of quilt

6. Measure the length of the quilt top and add 2". Cut two binding strips to this measurement. Pin the strips to the sides of the quilt front, aligning raw edges and leaving 1" extending beyond the top and bottom edges. Stitch the binding in place.

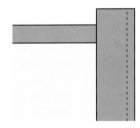

7. On each side, fold the binding up but not over the quilt edge. Fold the excess on each end of the strip over the top and bottom binding, and then fold the remainder of the binding to the back and pin it in place.

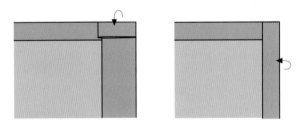

8. Hand stitch the folded edges of the binding in place on the back of the quilt, using an appliqué stitch or slip stitch.

Labeling

It is very important that you put a label or some kind of documentation on your quilt. This will help future generations give you proper credit when they are enjoying your skills a hundred years from now.

Every label should indicate, at the very least, your name and the date you finished the quilt. I also include the name of the quilt and my city and state. The label can contain as much information as you like. Some things that you might add are the occasion for which the quilt was made and, if it was a gift, to whom it was given. Some quilters have been known to put a few scraps of the fabrics used in the quilt behind the label. These scraps will fade at the same rate as the rest of the quilt, so if a repair is needed at a later date, the fabric will be readily available.

You can write your label information directly on the quilt backing with a permanent marker, or on a label that you hand appliqué to the backing. The label can be handwritten or computer generated. If you want to use your computer, cut an 8½" x 11" sheet of freezer paper and iron the label fabric to the waxy side. Trim the fabric to the same size as the paper so that you can run it through your laser ink-jet printer. This is a cheap version of photo-transfer paper. I wouldn't recommend this method for anything large or for multiple copies because the printer will sometimes pull the fabric and paper through at an angle, but it will work for a small label.

Over the past years, I have made high school graduation quilts for my nieces and nephews. As part of the backing, I piece their graduation year in large block-style numbers. At the graduation open house, the guests sign their good wishes on the numbers as sort of a guest book. When the young people go off to college, they take not only a warm and cozy quilt, but also the best wishes of their family and friends. I have also included photo-transfer pictures in some of my quilt labels. The backing of my parents' 50th anniversary quilt, shown below, included block-style numbers and photo-transfer pictures.

Back of "Golden Mimosa," page 50

PIÑA COLADA

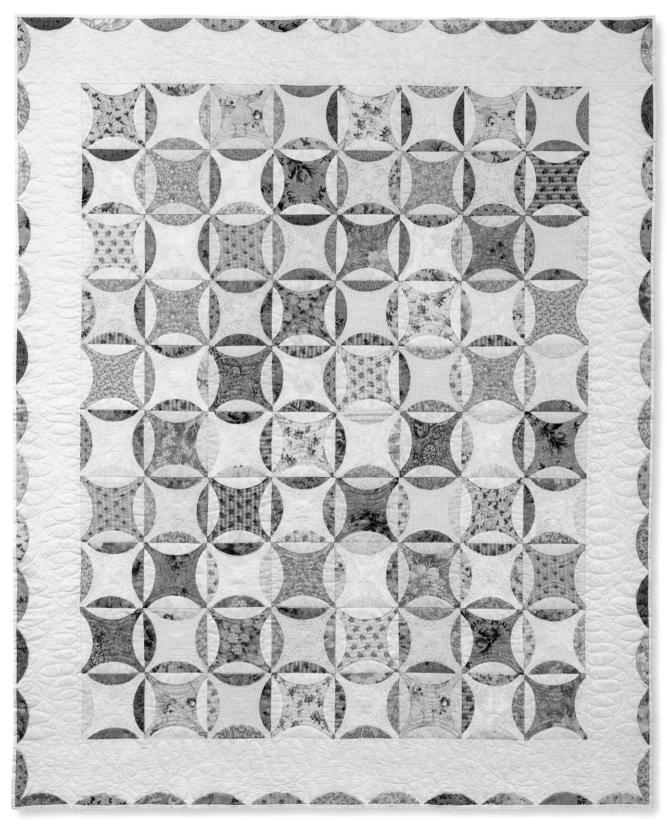

Finished Quilt: 60½" x 72½" • Finished Block: 6" x 6"

What better place than the beach to enjoy a warm breeze kissing your skin as you sip a cool piña colada? When that isn't possible, you can still evoke the relaxed mood and warm thoughts of paradise with this charming quilt made from soft pastel prints and creamy white fabric. Add a touch of fun by sewing three-dimensional curved pieces along the border edge to create an easy scalloped effect.

Piña Colada (frozen)

In blender:
½ cup of ice
2 oz light rum
2 tbsp cream of coconut
½ cup fresh or canned pineapple
1 tbsp vanilla ice cream (optional)
Blend until smooth.
If too thick add fruit or juice.
If too thin add ice or ice cream.
Garnish with pineapple and cherry.

MATERIALS

Yardages are based on 42"-wide fabrics.

3½ yards *total* of assorted light fabrics for blocks*

3½ yards *total* of assorted dark pastel fabrics for blocks and border*

2½ yards of white print for border and binding

4 yards of fabric for backing

64" x 76" piece of batting

2½ yards of 45"-wide lightweight nonfusible interfacing

Template plastic

Water-soluble marker

*Scraps can be used for some pieces but they need to be no smaller than 6½" square. You will also need several 2½"-wide full-width strips. Refer to the cutting instructions for specifics.

CUTTING

All measurements include ¼"-wide seam allowances. Cut all strips across the width of the fabric unless otherwise indicated.

From the interfacing, cut:
32 strips, 2½" x 45"

From the assorted lights, cut a *total* of:
21 strips, 2½" x 42"
40 squares, 6½" x 6½"

From the assorted dark pastels, cut a *total* of:
21 strips, 2½" x 42"
40 squares, 6½" x 6½"

From the *lengthwise* grain of the white print, cut:
4 strips, 6½" x 62"

From the remainder of the white print, cut:
7 binding strips, 3" x 42"

MAKING THE BLOCKS

1. Make a plastic template of the arc pattern on page 17.

2. Using the template, trace 160 shapes onto 16 interfacing strips, aligning the template straight edge with the interfacing long edges and tracing shapes along both sides of the strip as shown. Leave approximately ½" of space between shapes. *Do not* cut out the shapes.

3. With right sides up, pin a marked interfacing strip to 16 light strips. Sew on the marked lines, backstitching at the beginning and end of each seam.

4. Repeat steps 2 and 3 to trace 160 shapes onto the remaining interfacing strips and stitch them to 16 dark pastel strips.

5. Cut out the appliqué shapes, leaving ⅛" to ¼" for seam allowance. Turn the appliqués right side out. Smooth out the curves and finger-press the fabric slightly over the interfacing side so that the interfacing won't show on the finished quilt. Use an iron to press each shape from the fabric side.

6. Center and pin a light appliqué to each side of a dark pastel 6½" square, aligning the straight edges. Appliqué the curved edges of each shape in place, using a blanket stitch, blind hem stitch, or narrow zigzag stitch.

2. Refer to "Adding Borders" on page 9 to trim the white print 6½"-wide strips to the correct lengths and sew them to the quilt center.

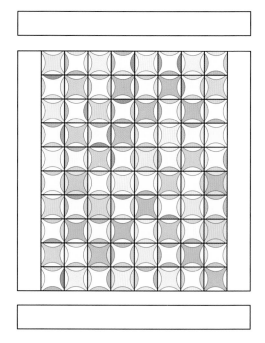

3. Using the appliqué template, trace a total of 48 shapes onto the wrong side of the remaining light strips. With right sides together, layer each light strip with a dark strip. Pin the strips together between the shapes. Sew on the marked lines. Cut out, turn, and press each shape as before.

4. With the dark side up, evenly space 13 shapes along the side borders, aligning the straight edges. Pin the shapes in place. Pin 11 shapes along the top and bottom borders in the same manner. Machine baste the shapes in place ⅛" from the border outer edges.

7. From the wrong side of the block, trim away the fabric and interfacing behind each appliqué, leaving ⅛" to ¼" for seam allowance and being careful not to cut into the top fabric.

8. Repeat steps 6 and 7 to appliqué the light shapes to each dark square and the dark shapes to each light square for a total of 80 blocks.

ASSEMBLING THE QUILT TOP

1. Arrange the blocks into 10 rows of eight blocks each, alternating the light and dark blocks in each row and from row to row. Sew the blocks in each row together. Press the seam allowances toward the light blocks. Sew the rows together. Press the seam allowances in one direction.

FINISHING THE QUILT

Refer to "Finishing Techniques" on pages 9–12 for detailed instructions.

1. Layer the quilt top, batting, and backing; baste the layers together.

2. Quilt in the ditch around each block to stabilize the quilt.

3. Drop the feed dogs and free-motion quilt along the curved edges of the block appliqués.

4. To quilt the light blocks, make a plastic template of the quilting pattern below right. Using a water-soluble marker, center the template on each light block and trace around it. Quilt on the traced lines. Fill in the light area around the template with stipple quilting.

    To quilt each dark block, echo quilt from the appliqué curved edges to the center.

5. Quilt a curved line down the center of each border and fill in with loops on each side of the line that go to the edge.

6. Bind the quilt with the white print 3"-wide strips.

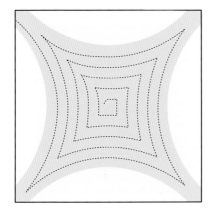

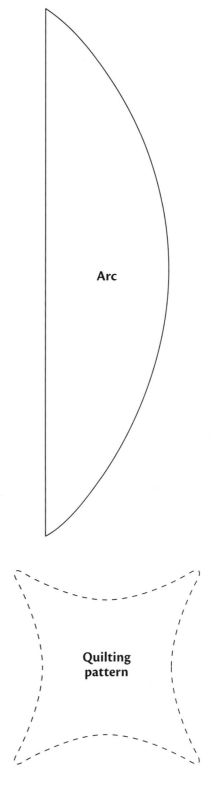

Arc

Quilting pattern

TEQUILA SUNRISE

Finished Quilt: 67¾" x 90¼" • **Finished Block:** 8" x 8"

Drink in the flavors of a tropical sunset as you bask in the warmth of this bed-sized quilt. Flavored with the citrusy colors of orange, lemon, and lime, the blocks are a tasty update of the Improved Nine Patch block.

MATERIALS

Yardages are based on 42"-wide fabrics.

4⅓ yards of bright multicolored print for blocks, setting triangles, outer border, and binding

2⅔ yards of green fabric for blocks

2 yards of dark orange fabric for blocks and inner border

1½ yards of yellow fabric for blocks

5½ yards of fabric for backing

71" x 94" piece of batting

2⅞ yards of 45"-wide lightweight nonfusible interfacing

Template plastic

CUTTING

All measurements include ¼"-wide seam allowances. Cut all strips across the width of the fabric.

From the green, cut:
22 strips, 3½" x 42"
4 strips, 2½" x 42"

From the bright multicolored print, cut:
11 strips, 2½" x 42"
8 strips, 3½" x 42"
2 strips, 12½" x 42"; crosscut into 5 squares, 12½" x 12½". Cut each square in half diagonally twice to yield 20 side setting triangles. From the remainder of one strip, cut 2 squares, 6½" x 6½"; cut each square in half diagonally to yield 4 corner setting triangles.
8 strips, 4½" x 42"
9 binding strips, 3" x 42"

From the interfacing, cut:
36 strips, 2½" x 45"

From the yellow, cut:
18 strips, 2½" x 42"

From the dark orange, cut:
18 strips, 2½" x 42"
8 strips, 2" x 42"

Tequila Sunrise

Fill a serving glass with ice.

Add 2 oz tequila.

Fill with orange juice.

Pour ½ oz grenadine down spoon
    to bottom of glass.

Garnish with orange.

Making the Blocks

1. Sew a green 3½" x 42" strip to both long edges of a multicolored print 2½" x 42" strip to make strip set A. Repeat to make a total of 11 strip sets. Press the seam allowances toward the green strips. Crosscut the strip sets into 118 segments, 3½" wide.

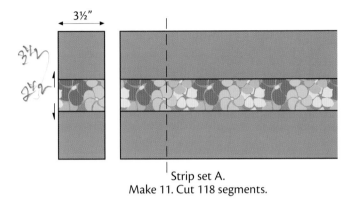

Strip set A.
Make 11. Cut 118 segments.

2. Sew a multicolored print 3½" x 42" strip to both long edges of a green 2½" x 42" strip to make strip set B. Repeat to make a total of four strip sets. Press the seam allowances toward the green strips. Crosscut the strip sets into 59 segments, 2½" wide.

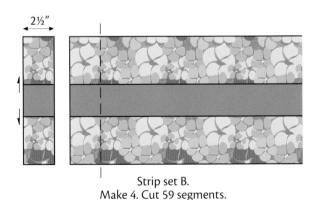

Strip set B.
Make 4. Cut 59 segments.

3. Sew an A segment to each side of a B segment to make a nine-patch unit. Press the seam allowances toward the A segments. Repeat to make a total of 59 units.

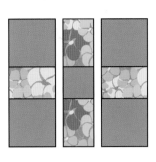
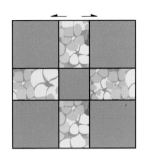

Make 59.

4. Make a plastic template of the arc pattern on page 23.

5. Using the template, trace 140 shapes onto 18 interfacing strips, aligning the template straight edge with the interfacing long edges and tracing shapes along both sides of the strip as shown. Leave approximately ½" of space between shapes. You should be able to fit approximately eight shapes per strip. *Do not* cut out the shapes.

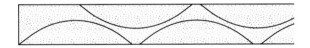

6. With right sides up, pin a marked interfacing strip to each yellow strip. Sew on the marked lines, backstitching at the beginning and end of each seam.

7. Repeat steps 5 and 6 to trace 140 shapes onto the remaining 18 interfacing strips and stitch them to the dark orange 2½" x 42" strips.

Assembling the Quilt Top

1. Center a dark orange appliqué on the short sides of each side setting triangle and the long side of each corner setting triangle and stitch them in place in the same manner as for the blocks.

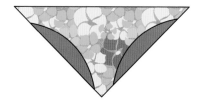 

8. Cut out the appliqué shapes, leaving ⅛" to ¼" for seam allowance. Turn the appliqués right side out. Smooth out the curves and finger-press the fabric slightly over the interfacing side so that the interfacing won't show on the finished quilt. Use an iron to press each shape from the fabric side.

9. Center and pin a yellow appliqué to each side of a nine-patch unit, aligning the straight edges. Appliqué the curved edges of each shape in place, using a blanket stitch, blind hem stitch, or narrow zigzag stitch. Repeat to make a total of 35 blocks. Repeat with the dark orange appliqués and the remaining nine-patch units to make 24 blocks. Set aside the remaining dark orange appliqués for the setting triangles.

2. Lay out the blocks and setting triangles in diagonal rows as shown, alternating the yellow and orange blocks in each row and from row to row. Sew the blocks and setting triangles in each row together, matching the appliqués. Press the seam allowances in opposite directions from row to row. Sew the rows together. Press the seam allowances away from the center row. Add the remaining corner setting triangles. Press the seam allowances toward the triangles.

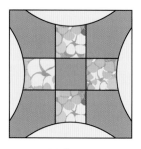 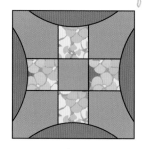

Make 35.   Make 24.

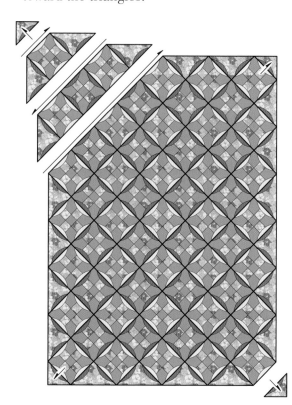

10. From the wrong side of the block, trim away the fabric and interfacing behind each appliqué, leaving ⅛" to ¼" for seam allowance and being careful not to cut into the top fabrics.

3. Refer to "Adding Borders" on page 9 to sew the dark orange 2"-wide border strips to the quilt center. Repeat to add the multicolored print 4½"-wide outer border.

Finishing the Quilt

Refer to "Finishing Techniques" on pages 9–12 for detailed instructions.

1. Layer the quilt top, batting, and backing; baste the layers together.

2. Quilt in the ditch between all the blocks and between the borders to stabilize the quilt.

3. Drop the feed dogs and free-motion quilt along the curved edges of the appliqués.

4. Quilt the blocks with the design shown. Echo quilt the setting triangles.

5. I quilted the inner border with a wave design and quilted the outer border with a repeating series of three arc shapes nested together.

6. Bind the quilt with the multicolored print 3"-wide strips.

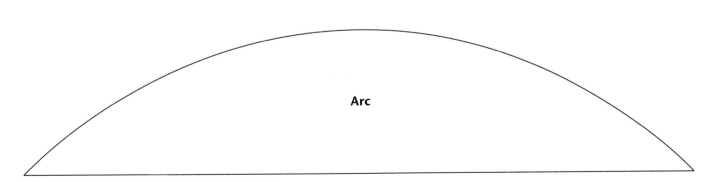

Arc

GREEN MOUNTAIN MELON

Finished Quilt: 66½" x 81" • **Finished Block: 10¼" x 10¼"**

Green Mountain Melon

Fill a tall glass with ice.
1 oz vodka
½ oz melon liqueur
1 oz lime juice
Fill with sour mix.
Shake.
Garnish with lime.

Throw out the notion that this quilt is too complex to make; the interfacing technique will have you tipsy with excitement and your friends green with envy at how quickly the blocks for this quilt can be completed. The block is versatile, too. Make just one quarter of it and then set it on point for a cute heart.

MATERIALS

Yardages are based on 42″-wide fabrics.

3⅝ yards of dark green for setting blocks, setting triangles, border, and binding
1 fat quarter OR ¼ yard *each* of at least 10 different assorted light to medium peach prints for main blocks*
1 fat quarter OR ¼ yard *each* of at least 10 different assorted dark green prints for main blocks*
1⅓ yards of white print for setting blocks and setting triangles
71" x 85" piece of batting
4 yards of fabric for backing
1½ yards of 45"-wide lightweight nonfusible interfacing
Template plastic
Each fat quarter or ¼-yard cut will yield pieces for two blocks. For more variety, use more fabrics.

CUTTING

All measurements include ¼″-wide seam allowances. Refer to the diagram on page 27 when cutting the peach and green pieces. Cut all strips across the width of the fabric.

From the assorted peach prints, cut 20 sets, with each set cut from the same fabric and consisting of:
2 squares, 6" x 6"; cut each square in half diagonally to yield 4 triangles
1 piece, 3½" x 15"

From the assorted green prints, cut 20 sets, with each set cut from the same fabric and consisting of:
2 squares, 6" x 6"; cut each square in half diagonally to yield 4 triangles
1 piece, 3½" x 15"

From the interfacing, cut:
14 strips, 3½" x 45"; crosscut into 40 pieces, 3½" x 15"

From the white print, cut:
3 strips, 6¾" x 42"; crosscut into 12 squares, 6¾" x 6¾"
2 strips, 10¾" x 42"; crosscut into 4 squares, 10¾" x 10¾". Cut each square in half diagonally twice to yield 16 side setting triangles (you'll have 2 triangles left over).
2 squares, 5¼" x 5¼"; cut each square in half diagonally to yield 4 corner setting triangles

Cutting the Peach and Green Pieces

Follow the diagrams to cut enough pieces for two blocks from each fat quarter or ¼-yard cut.

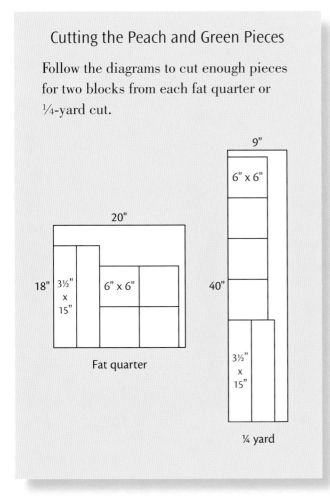

Fat quarter

¼ yard

From the dark green, cut:

21 strips, 2½" x 42"; crosscut into:
- 24 pieces, 2½" x 6¾"
- 24 pieces, 2½" x 10¾"
- 14 pieces, 2½" x 10"
- 14 pieces, 2½" x 11½"
- 4 pieces, 2½" x 12"

8 strips, 4½" x 42"

8 binding strips, 3" x 42"

MAKING THE MAIN BLOCKS

1. Make a plastic template of the scallop pattern on page 29.

2. Using the template, trace four shapes onto each interfacing piece. Leave approximately ½" of space between shapes. *Do not* cut out the shapes.

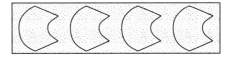

3. With right sides up, pin a marked interfacing piece to the 3½" x 15" strip from a peach set. Sew on the *curved* lines, backstitching at the beginning and end of each seam and leaving the sides open.

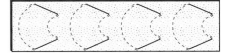

4. Cut out the appliqué shapes, leaving ⅛" to ¼" for seam allowance along the stitched edges and cutting directly on the line along the sides. Clip the curves. Turn the appliqués right side out. Smooth out the curves and finger-press the fabric slightly over the interfacing side so that the interfacing won't show on the finished quilt. Use an iron to press each shape from the fabric side. Return the appliqués to the set.

5. Repeat steps 3 and 4 with the 3½" x 15" pieces from each peach and green set.

6. Select one peach and one green set. Pin a peach appliqué from the set to each green triangle as shown, aligning the appliqué straight edges with the long edge and one short edge of the triangle. Pin a green appliqué from the set to each peach triangle as shown. Appliqué the curved edges of each appliqué in place, using a blanket stitch, blind hem stitch, or narrow zigzag stitch.

7. From the wrong side of each triangle, trim away the fabric and interfacing behind each appliqué, leaving ⅛" to ¼" for seam allowance and being careful not to cut into the triangle fabric.

8. Sew each peach triangle to a green triangle to form a square. Press the seam allowances toward the green triangles. Lay out the squares in two rows of two squares each so that the colors alternate around the square. Sew the squares in each row together. Press the seam allowances in opposite directions. Sew the rows together. Press the seam allowance in either direction.

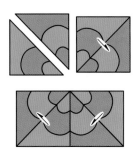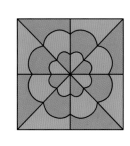

9. Repeat steps 6–8 to make a total of 20 blocks.

Making the Setting Blocks and Triangles

1. To make the setting blocks, sew dark green 2½" x 6¾" pieces to opposite sides of a white print 6¾" square. Press the seam allowances toward the green pieces. Add dark green 2½" x 10¾" pieces to the remaining sides. Press the seam allowances toward the green pieces. Repeat to make a total of 12 blocks.

Make 12.

2. To make the side setting triangles, sew a dark green 2½" x 10" piece to one short edge of each white print 10¾" triangle as shown. The green pieces are longer than necessary and will extend beyond the long edge of the triangles. Press the seam allowances toward the green pieces. Sew a 2½" x 11½" piece to the remaining short edge of each triangle, aligning the top of the green pieces with the side of the already joined green pieces. Press the seam allowances toward the green pieces.

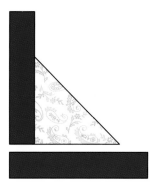

3. Trim the ends of the green strips even with the long edge of each triangle.

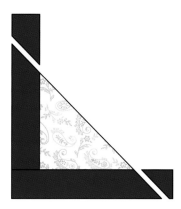

4. To make the corner setting triangles, center and sew a dark green 2½" x 12" piece to the long edge of each white print 5¼" triangle. Trim the green strips even with the short edges of the triangles.

Assembling the Quilt Top

1. Lay out the blocks and setting triangles in diagonal rows. Join the pieces in each row. The side setting triangles are larger than necessary, so you will need to align the corner of the triangle with the bottom edge of the main blocks, sew them in place, and then trim the excess even with the top of the blocks. Press the seam allowances toward the setting pieces. Join the rows. Press the seam allowances away from the center row. Add the remaining corner setting triangles. Press the seam allowances toward the triangles. Trim the excess side setting triangles ¼" from the block points.

2. Refer to "Adding Borders" on page 9 to sew the dark green 4½"-wide border strips to the quilt center.

Finishing the Quilt

Refer to "Finishing Techniques" on pages 9–12 for detailed instructions.

1. Layer the quilt top, batting, and backing; baste the layers together.

2. Quilt in the ditch between all the blocks to stabilize the quilt.

3. Drop the feed dogs and free-motion quilt along the curved edges of the appliqués. Echo quilt three lines on each appliqué.

4. Stipple quilt the background of the main blocks.

5. Quilt the setting blocks with a design similar to the one shown.

6. Quilt a zigzag design through the dark green strips of the setting blocks and setting triangles. Also quilt a zigzag design across the width of the border.

7. Bind the quilt using the dark green 3"-wide strips.

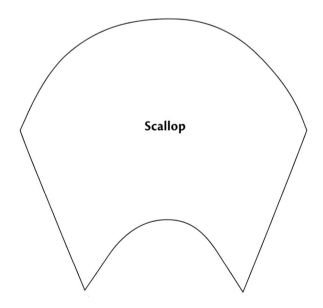

Scallop

STINGER

Finished Quilt: 68½" x 68½" • Finished Block: 12¼" x 12¼"

Blend a variety of black-and-white prints with a generous assortment of yellow fabrics and you've got a quilt that's buzzing with excitement. Keep the quilt from being too busy by using the same two fabrics for the block appliqués, and be sure the fabrics you select for the border appliqués provide enough contrast against the background fabric.

MATERIALS

Yardages are based on 42"-wide fabrics.

2⅝ yards of black solid for block appliqués, inner border, outer-border vine appliqué, and binding

2¼ yards of black-on-white print 1 for outer border

2¼ yards *total* of assorted yellow prints for blocks and outer-border large flower appliqués

2 yards *total* of assorted black-and-white prints for blocks and outer-border appliqués*

⅞ yard of black-on-white print 2 for block appliqués

¼ yard of black-on-white print 3 for outer-border flower center appliqués

¼ yard of yellow print for outer-border small flower appliqués

4 yards of fabric for backing

73" x 73" piece of batting

2½ yards of 45"-wide lightweight nonfusible interfacing

Template plastic

Water-soluble marker

The majority of the prints should be white-on-black prints, but be sure to use a few black-on-white prints as well.

CUTTING

All measurements include ¼"-wide seam allowances. Cut all strips across the width of the fabric unless otherwise indicated.

From the interfacing, cut:

16 strips, 2½" x 45"

3 strips, 5" x 45"; cut each strip in half crosswise to yield 6 pieces, 5" x 22½". You will use 5 and have 1 extra.

3 strips, 4¾" x 45"; crosscut into 20 squares, 4¾" x 4¾"

1 strip, 3¾" x 45"

2 strips, 3¼" x 45"

From black-on-white print 2, cut:

16 strips, 1½" x 42"

From the black solid, cut:

16 strips, 1½" x 42"

6 strips, 2" x 42"

8 binding strips, 3" x 42"

From the assorted yellow prints, cut a *total* of:

16 pairs of squares (32 total), 7" x 7"; cut each square in half diagonally to yield 64 triangles

5 pieces, 5" x 21"

Stinger

Fill a short glass with ice.
1½ oz brandy
½ oz white crème de menthe
Stir.
Serve or strain into chilled glass.

From the assorted black-and-white prints, cut a *total* of:

16 pairs of squares (32 total), 7" x 7"; cut each square in half diagonally to yield 64 triangles

20 squares, 4¾" x 4¾" (use white-on-black prints only)

From black-on-white print 3, cut:

1 strip, 3¾" x 42"

From the yellow print for small flower appliqués, cut:

2 strips, 3¼" x 42"

From the *lengthwise* grain of black-on-white print 1, cut:

2 strips, 8½" x 55"
2 strips, 8½" x 72"

MAKING THE BLOCKS

1. Make a plastic template of the leaf pattern on page 37. Transfer the center line to the template.

2. Draw a line through the lengthwise center of each 2½"-wide interfacing strip. Using the template, trace eight shapes onto *each* interfacing strip (128 total), matching up the center line on the template with the line on the interfacing and leaving approximately ½" of space between shapes. *Do not* cut out the shapes.

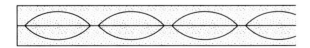

3. Using the 1½" x 42" strips, sew each black-on-white print 2 strip to a black solid strip along the long edges. Press the seam allowances open.

4. With right sides up, pin a marked interfacing strip to each joined strip from step 3, matching up the center line on the interfacing with the strip seam line. Sew on the marked lines, slightly overlapping the stitching at the beginning and end of each seam.

5. Cut out the appliqué shapes, leaving ⅛" to ¼" for seam allowance. Cut a slit in the interfacing of each shape and turn the appliqués right side out. Use a turning tool to push out the seams and points. Finger-press the fabric slightly over the interfacing side so that the interfacing won't show on the finished quilt. Use an iron to press each shape from the fabric side. Set the appliqués aside.

6. Sew four matching yellow triangles to four matching black-and-white triangles along the long edges to make four pieced squares.

Make 4.

7. Arrange the pieced squares into two rows of two squares each. Join the squares in each row. Press the seam allowances in opposite directions. Join the rows. Press the seam allowance in either direction.

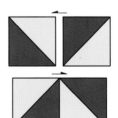 

8. Repeat steps 6 and 7 to make a total of 16 block background squares.

9. Fold each corner of the block background squares into the center and finger-press the folds.

10. Turn back the folded corners and pin two appliqué pieces ¼" in from each fold as shown, alternating the placement of the colors.

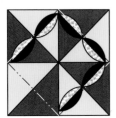 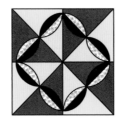

11. Appliqué each shape in place, using a blanket stitch, blind hem stitch, or narrow zigzag stitch. *Do not* trim away the fabric and interfacing behind each appliqué.

ASSEMBLING THE QUILT TOP

1. Lay out the blocks in four rows of four blocks each. Sew the blocks in each row together. Press the seam allowances in opposite directions from row to row. Sew the rows together. Press the seam allowances in one direction.

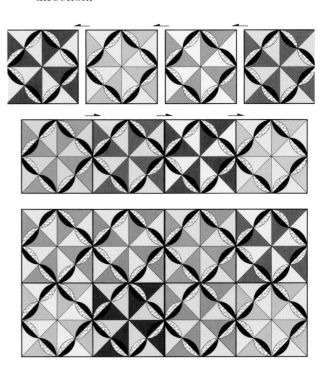

2. Refer to "Adding Borders" on page 9 to add the black solid 2"-wide border strips to the quilt center.

3. Make plastic templates for the small flower, large flower, and flower center appliqué shapes, using the patterns on page 37.

4. Using the large flower template, trace four shapes onto each 5" x 22½" interfacing piece (20 total). On the 4¾" squares of interfacing, use the block appliqué and border leaf template to trace two shapes onto *each* square. You do not need to transfer the center line to the shapes. Trace the flower center template onto the 3¾" x 45" interfacing strip 20 times. Use the small flower template to trace 12 shapes onto the 3¼" x 45" interfacing strips.

Leave approximately ½" of space between shapes. *Do not* cut out the shapes.

Large flower arrangement

Leaf arrangement

Flower center arrangement

Small flower arrangement

5. With right sides up, pin the large flower interfacing strips to the assorted yellow 5" x 21" pieces, a leaf interfacing square to each black-and-white print 4¾" square, the flower center interfacing strip to the black-on-white print 3 strip, and the small flower interfacing strips to the yellow 3¼" x 42" strips. Sew on the marked line of each shape, slightly overlapping the stitching at the beginning and end of each seam.

6. Cut out the appliqué shapes, leaving at least ⅛" for a seam allowance. Clip the inside points of the flower shapes. Cut a slit in the interfacing of each shape and turn the appliqués right side out. Use a turning tool to smooth out the curves and push out the points. Finger-press the fabric slightly over the interfacing side so that the interfacing won't show on the finished quilt. Use an iron to press each shape from the fabric side.

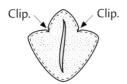

Clip.   Clip.

7. Position a flower center appliqué on each large flower as shown and appliqué it in place,

using a blanket stitch, blind hem stitch, or narrow zigzag stitch. Trim away the fabric and interfacing behind each flower center appliqué, if desired.

8. Refer to "Cutting Bias Strips" on page 8 to cut 1¼"-wide bias strips from the remaining black solid fabric for the vines. You will need eight 21"-long segments and eight 16"-long segments. Piece strips together and trim them as needed to achieve the required lengths. Fold each segment in half, wrong sides together. Sew ⅛" from the raw edges of each strip. Center the seam under each segment and press it flat.

9. Center an 8½" x 72" black-on-white print 1 strip along the top edge of the assembled quilt top. The strip center should align with the seam line that joins the second and third blocks. With the water-soluble marker, make a mark 1¼" from the top edge of the border strip at the center point. Place the center tip of a small flower at the mark and pin the appliqué in place. Repeat to position and pin a small flower 1¼" from the top edge of the border strip on each side of the center flower, aligning them with the seam lines joining the first and second blocks and the third and fourth blocks.

   Curve a 16"-long vine segment between each small flower, tucking the ends under the appliqués so they are slightly to the sides of the flower bottom point. Pin the vines in place so that the lowest point of the curves is at the center of the blocks and 1¼" from the bottom edge of the border strip. Use a dinner plate to help you with the curves, if necessary.

Pin a large flower at the bottom of each vine curve, centering each one with the center of the block below it. Refer to the photo to tuck two matching leaves under the sides of each large flower and pin them in place.

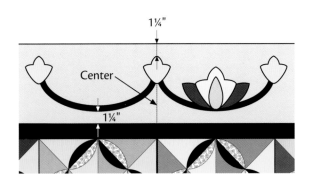

10. Make a mark 1¼" from the lower edge of the border at the center point of the first and fourth blocks. Tuck the end of a 21"-long vine segment under the outer sides of the first and last small flower. Curve the vine toward the bottom edge of the border, pinning it in place just up to the mark. Leave the remainder of the vine unattached. Add the large flower and leaves in the same manner as before.

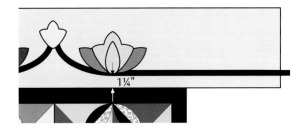

11. Appliqué the border pieces in place, using a blanket stitch, blind hem stitch, or narrow zigzag stitch. Leave the ends of the long vines at each end of the border unattached.

12. Repeat steps 9–11 for the other three borders, using the remaining black-on-white print 8½" x 72" strip for the bottom border and the 8½" x 55" strips for the side borders.

13. Sew the side borders to the quilt top, matching the border and quilt centers. Trim the ends of the borders even with the quilt top and bottom edges. Add the top and bottom borders, matching centers. Trim the ends of the borders even with the quilt sides.

14. Pin a large flower and two leaves in each corner of the quilt as shown. Tuck the ends of the unattached vines under the flower as before. Appliqué the pieces in place. If desired, trim away the fabric and interfacing behind each appliqué, leaving ⅛" to ¼" for seam allowance.

Finishing the Quilt

Refer to "Finishing Techniques" on pages 9–12 for detailed instructions.

1. Layer the quilt top, batting, and backing; baste the layers together.

2. Quilt in the ditch around each block to stabilize the quilt.

3. Drop the feed dogs and free-motion quilt along the curved edges of the block appliqués.

4. In the block backgrounds, echo quilt around the appliqués.

5. In the border, outline quilt around the appliquéd vine and flowers and then stipple quilt in the background of the border.

6. Bind the quilt with the black solid 3"-wide strips.

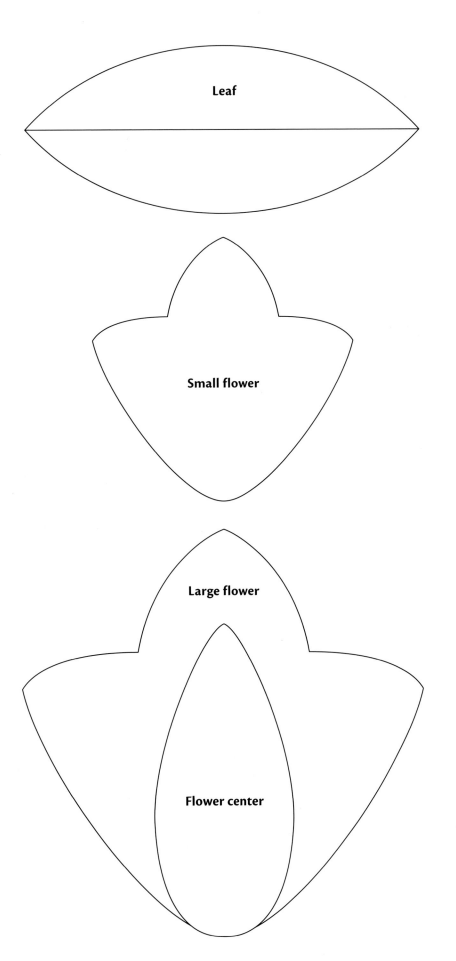

Leaf

Small flower

Large flower

Flower center

LARGE STARBURST

Finished Quilt: 88½" x 98½"

If you're looking for a fast and easy large quilt, you've turned to the right page. You'll find the star-shaped flowers quick to make, plus they're great for using up your larger scraps. For a smaller version without the borders, see "Small Starburst" on page 46.

MATERIALS

Yardages are based on 42"-wide fabrics.

7½ yards of cream print for panel backgrounds, outer border, and binding

2⅞ yards *total* OR 12 fat quarters of assorted coordinating prints for flower appliqués

2¼ yards of medium green print for sashing and inner border

2 yards of dark green print for leaf and vine appliqués

¼ yard *each* of dark brown print and gold print for flower center appliqués

8 yards of fabric for backing

93" x 103" piece of batting

3⅝ yards of 45"-wide lightweight nonfusible interfacing

Template plastic

Water-soluble marker

CUTTING

All measurements include ¼"-wide seam allowances. Cut all strips across the width of the fabric unless otherwise indicated.

From the interfacing, cut:
10 strips, 7¾" x 45"
10 strips, 3⅛" x 45"
4 strips, 2½" x 45"

From the dark green print, cut:
9 strips, 3⅛" x 42"

From *each* of the dark brown and gold prints, cut:
2 strips, 2½" x 42"

From the *lengthwise* grain of the cream print, cut:
5 strips, 10½" x 72½"
2 strips, 10½" x 81"
2 strips, 10½" x 91"

From the *lengthwise* grain of the medium green print, cut:
6 strips, 3½" x 72½"
2 strips, 3½" x 68½"

From the remainder of the medium green print, cut:
10 squares, 6½" x 6½"; cut each square in half diagonally to yield 20 triangles

Starburst

Fill a mixing glass with ice.

3½ oz citrus vodka or citrus rum

½ oz amaretto

1 oz cranberry juice

Shake.

Strain into chilled glass.

LARGE STARBURST

MAKING THE APPLIQUÉS

1. Make plastic templates for the flower, flower center, and leaf appliqué shapes, using the patterns on page 45.

2. Using the flower template, trace 65 shapes onto the 7¾"-wide interfacing strips. Leave approximately ½" of space between shapes. You should be able to fit approximately seven shapes per strip. Cut the strips apart between the shapes, leaving at least a ¼" margin of interfacing.

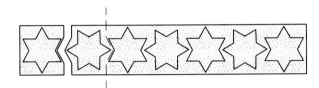

3. Use the leaf template to trace 188 shapes onto the 3⅛"-wide interfacing strips. You should be able to fit approximately 20 shapes per strip. Trace the flower center template onto the 2½"-wide interfacing strips a total of 65 times. Leave approximately ½" of space between shapes. *Do not* cut out the shapes.

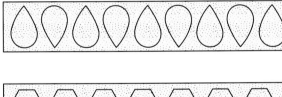

4. With right sides up, pin each interfacing flower shape to an assorted coordinating print fabric or fat quarter, the leaf interfacing strips to the dark green print strips, and the flower center interfacing strips to the dark brown and gold print strips. Sew on the marked lines, slightly overlapping the stitching at the beginning and end of each seam.

5. Cut out the appliqué shapes, leaving ⅛" to ¼" for seam allowance. Clip the inner points of the flower shapes. Cut a slit in the interfacing of each shape and turn the appliqués right side out. Use a turning tool to push out the points. Finger-press the fabric slightly over the interfacing side so that the interfacing won't show on the finished quilt. Use an iron to press each shape from the fabric side.

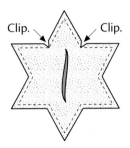

Clip.   Clip.

6. Center a flower center appliqué on each flower and appliqué it in place, using a blanket stitch, blind hem stitch, or narrow zigzag stitch. If desired, trim away the backing and interfacing behind the center appliqué, leaving ⅛" to ¼" for seam allowance and being careful not to cut into the top fabric.

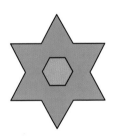

7. Refer to "Cutting Bias Strips" on page 8 to cut 1¼"-wide bias strips from the remainder of the dark green print for the vines. You will need 52 segments, 8½" long, and 8 segments, 12" long. Fold each segment in half, wrong sides together. Sew ⅛" from the raw edges of each segment. Center the seam under each segment and press it flat.

MAKING THE APPLIQUÉ PANELS

1. Draw a 45°-angle line across all four corners of each cream 10½" x 72½" strip, marking from the center of the top and bottom edges to the sides.

2. For each panel, with right sides together, center the long edge of a medium green triangle on one drawn line. Stitch ¼" from the triangle long edge. Press the green triangle toward the corner of the cream strip. Repeat on the opposite corner, and then repeat the process on the opposite end.

3. Trim the triangle raw edges even with the background strips. Cut away the background fabric under each triangle.

4. Pin seven flower appliqués to the center of each strip, positioning the first and last flowers 2" from the ends and spacing the remaining flowers approximately 3¼" apart.

5. Using the water-soluble marker and a small plate, draw a curve for the vine placement between each appliqué as shown, starting on the left side of each panel and alternating sides each time.

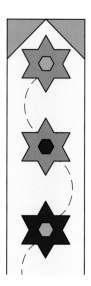

6. With the seam side down, pin the 8½" vine segments over each drawn curve. Tuck the ends of the vines under the flowers. Pin three leaves between each flower as shown.

7. Appliqué the shapes on each panel in place, using a blanket stitch, blind hem stitch, or narrow zigzag stitch. If desired, trim away the fabric and interfacing behind each flower and leaf appliqué, leaving ⅛" to ¼" for seam allowance and being careful not to cut into the top fabrics.

Assembling the Quilt Top

1. Sew the appliquéd panels and medium green 3½" x 72½" strips together side by side along the long edges as shown. Press the seam allowances toward the green strips. Add the medium green 3½" x 68½" strips to the top and bottom of the panel unit. Press the seam allowances toward the top and bottom borders.

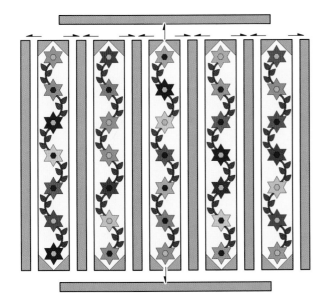

2. Measure the length of the quilt top through the center. Trim the cream 10½" x 81" strips to the exact length measured. Position the borders next to the sides of the assembled quilt top. Pin seven flower appliqués into place on each border, centering them on the strips and positioning them so they are in line with each horizontal row of flowers on the panels. Mark the vine placement between the flowers as you did for the panels, and then pin the vines and leaves into place. Appliqué

the pieces in place. Sew the borders to the sides of the quilt.

3. Measure the width of the quilt top, including the side borders. Trim the cream 10½" x 91" strips to the exact length measured. Position the borders next to the top and bottom edges of the quilt top. Pin six flower appliqués into place on each border, centering them on the strip. Position the first and last flowers so they are in line with each vertical row of flowers on the panels. Space the remaining appliqués approximately 3½" apart. Mark the vine placement between the flowers as you did for the panels, and then pin the 8½"-long vines and leaves into place. Appliqué the pieces in place. Sew the borders to the top and bottom edges of the quilt.

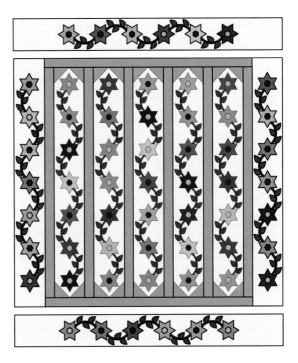

4. Pin a flower appliqué in each corner of the outer border, positioning them so they are in line vertically and horizontally with the other flowers. Draw the vine placement lines from each corner flower to the adjacent border flowers. Pin the 12"-long vine segments in place and then add the leaves as shown. Appliqué the pieces in place.

5. If desired, trim away the interfacing and background fabric behind each flower and leaf appliqué, leaving ⅛" to ¼" for seam allowance and being careful not to cut into the top fabrics.

Finishing the Quilt

Refer to "Finishing Techniques" on pages 9–12 for detailed instructions.

1. Layer the quilt top, batting, and backing; baste the layers together.

2. Quilt in the ditch between the panels and the sashing and inner-border strips to stabilize the quilt.

3. Drop the feed dogs and free-motion outline quilt around the flowers, leaves, vines, and flower centers. Quilt the design shown on the flower template onto the flowers.

4. Stipple quilt in the background of each panel.

5. For the top and bottom inner border, quilt V-shaped parallel lines 1" apart. Quilt a border design into the sashing strips and inner side borders.

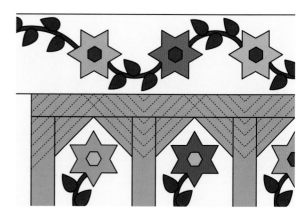

6. Stipple quilt the background of the outer border.

7. From the remainder of the cream print, cut enough 3"-wide strips along the lengthwise grain to equal 385" when sewn together. Sew the strips together end to end and press the seam allowances open. Bind the quilt.

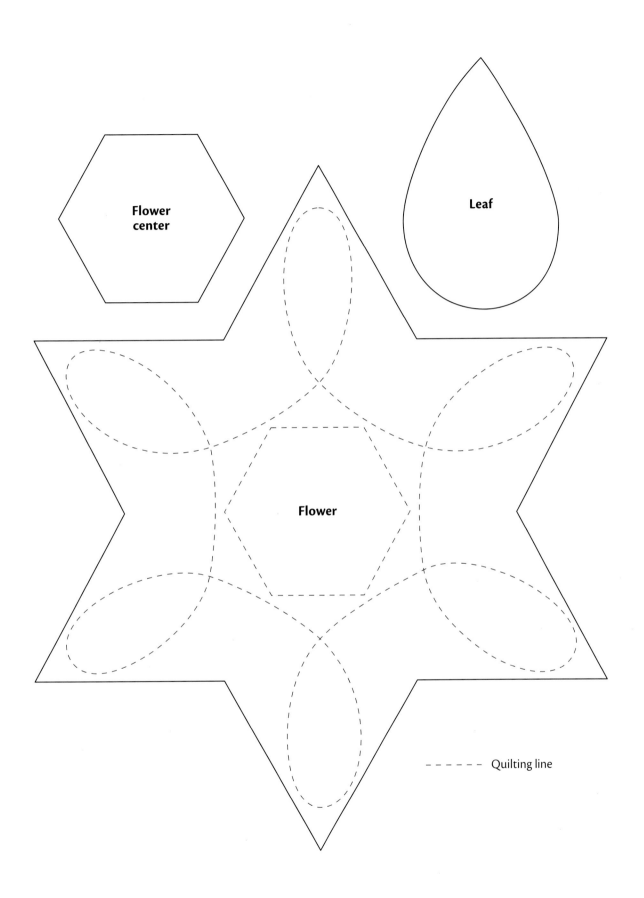

Flower center

Leaf

Flower

— — — Quilting line

SMALL STARBURST

Finished Quilt: 55½" x 66½"

I made the original version of this project from flannel fabrics for my personal snuggle quilt. Although this quilt isn't flannel, it's just as nice as the original for wrapping up in and enjoying a good book and a favorite beverage.

MATERIALS

Yardages are based on 42"-wide fabrics.

3⅔ yards of cream print for panel backgrounds and flower center appliqués*

2½ yards of dark brown print for sashing, border, and binding

1¼ yards *total* OR 5 fat quarters of assorted medium to dark pink prints for flower appliqués

1 yard of light brown print for leaf and vine appliqués

¼ yard of dark pink print for flower inner center appliqués

4 yards of fabric for backing

60" x 71" piece of batting

1¾ yards of 45"-wide lightweight nonfusible interfacing

If your fabric is more than 42" wide, you will need only 2 yards.

CUTTING

All measurements include ¼"-wide seam allowances. Cut all strips across the width of the fabric unless otherwise indicated.

From the interfacing, cut:
4 strips, 7¾" x 45"
4 strips, 3⅛" x 45"
2 strips, 2½" x 45"
2 strips, 1¾" x 45"

From the dark pink print for flower inner center appliqués, cut:
2 strips, 1¾" x 42"

From the *lengthwise* grain of the cream print, cut:
4 strips, 10½" x 60½"
2 strips, 2½" x 45"

From the *lengthwise* grain of the dark brown print, cut:
5 strips, 3½" x 60½"
2 strips, 3½" x 57"
3 binding strips, 3" x length of fabric

From the remainder of the dark brown print, cut:
8 squares, 6½" x 6½"; cut each square in half diagonally to yield 16 triangles

From the light brown print, cut:
4 strips, 3⅛" x 42"

Rosé Cooler

Fill a wine glass ¾ with ice.

Fill ¾ with rosé wine.

Fill with ginger ale or lemon-lime soda.

Garnish with lime.

QUILT ASSEMBLY

1. Referring to page 41 of "Large Starburst," follow steps 1–5 of "Making the Appliqués" to make 24 flowers from the assorted pink prints, 24 outer flower centers from the cream print 2½" x 45" strips, and 60 leaves from the light brown print.

2. Make a plastic template for the flower inner center, using the pattern at right. Use the template to trace 24 shapes onto the 1¾" x 45" interfacing strips and make the appliqués from the dark pink strips in the same manner as the shapes in step 1.

3. Center a flower center appliqué on each flower and appliqué it in place, using a blanket stitch, blind hem stitch, or narrow zigzag stitch. If desired, trim away the fabric and interfacing behind the center appliqué, leaving ⅛" to ¼" for seam allowance and being careful not to cut into the top fabric. Center a flower inner center appliqué on each flower center appliqué. Appliqué the shapes in place as before and trim away the flower center fabric and interfacing behind each piece, if desired.

4. Follow step 7 of "Making the Appliqués" to make 20 vine segments, 8½" long, from the remainder of the light brown fabric.

5. Make four panels as described on page 42 in "Making the Appliqué Panels," using six flowers and positioning the first and last flowers 1¾" from the ends and the remaining flowers 3" apart.

6. Refer to step 1 of "Assembling the Quilt Top" on page 43 to sew the panels and 3½" x 60½" dark brown sashing and border strips together to complete the quilt top. Follow step 3 to add the top and bottom borders, trimming the dark brown 3½" x 57" strips to the exact length. Finish as instructed for the larger quilt.

**Flower
inner
center**

GOLDEN MIMOSA

Finished Quilt: 58" x 69"

Special occasions are ideal for commemorating with gifts from the heart. To adorn this lap-sized quilt, I appliquéd dozens of leaves cut from a variety of gold fabrics in celebration of the 50th anniversary of my parents' fall wedding.

MATERIALS

Yardages are based on 42″-wide fabrics.

4½ yards of cream print for center panel and outer border*

⅛ yard *each* of 15 assorted gold fabrics for leaf appliqués

1 yard of gold print for vine appliqués

½ yard of gold fabric for inner border

⅔ yard of fabric for binding

3½ yards of fabric for backing

62" x 73" piece of batting

1¾ yards of 45"-wide lightweight nonfusible interfacing

Template plastic

*If your fabric is more than 42″ wide, you will need only 3¼ yards.

CUTTING

All measurements include ¼″-wide seam allowances. Cut all strips across the width of the fabric unless otherwise indicated.

From the interfacing, cut:
15 strips, 3¾" x 45"

From *each* of the assorted gold fabrics for leaf appliqués, cut:
1 strip, 3¾" x 42" (15 total)

From the cream print, cut:
1 rectangle, 33" x 44"

From the *lengthwise* grain of the remainder of the cream print, cut:
2 strips, 10½" x 62"
2 strips, 10½" x 52"

From the gold fabric for inner border, cut:
5 strips, 3" x 42"

From the binding fabric, cut:
7 strips, 3" x 42"

MAKING THE APPLIQUÉS

1. Make a plastic template of the leaf pattern on page 54.

2. Using the template, trace 20 shapes onto each interfacing strip (300 shapes total). Leave approximately ½" of space between shapes. *Do not* cut out the shapes.

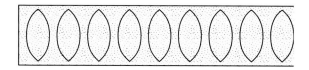

3. With right sides up, pin a marked interfacing strip to each assorted gold fabric strip. Sew on the marked lines, slightly overlapping the stitching at the beginning and end of each seam.

Grand Mimosa

Fill a serving glass with ice.

Fill ¾ with champagne.

Dash of orange liqueur

Fill with orange juice.

Garnish with orange.

4. Cut out the leaves, leaving ⅛" to ¼" for seam allowance. Cut a slit in the interfacing of each shape and turn the appliqués right side out. Use a turning tool to smooth the curves and push out the points. Finger-press the fabric slightly over the interfacing side so that the interfacing won't show on the finished quilt. Use an iron to press each leaf from the fabric side.

5. Refer to "Cutting Bias Strips" on page 8 to cut approximately 332" of 1¼"-wide bias strips from the vine fabric. Join the strips end to end at a 45° angle to make one strip approximately 112" long and another approximately 220" long.

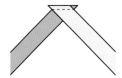

6. Fold each vine length in half, wrong sides together. Sew ⅛" from the raw edges of each length. With the seam centered on the underside, press the vines flat.

Assembling and Appliquéing the Quilt Top

1. Arrange and pin the shorter vine length, seam side down, on the cream rectangle as shown. Make sure the sides are symmetrical and the top and bottom are symmetrical.

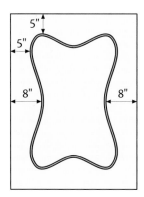

2. Appliqué the vine in place, using a blanket stitch, blind hem stitch, or narrow zigzag stitch.

3. Pin approximately 100 leaf appliqués to the vine. The arrangement of the leaves on the quilt shown is very uniform, but a more random placement of the leaves would be acceptable as well. Appliqué the leaves in place.

4. Refer to "Adding Borders" on page 9 to sew the gold 3"-wide border strips to the sides and then the top and bottom edges of the appliquéd rectangle, piecing the strips as necessary. Add the cream 10½"-wide outer-border strips to the quilt top, using the longer strips for the sides and trimming the strips to the exact lengths needed.

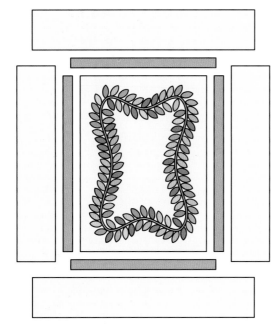

5. Arrange and pin the remaining vine length, seam side down, to the outer border so that it is symmetrical. Appliqué the vine in place. Pin the remaining leaves to the vine and appliqué them in place.

Finishing the Quilt

Refer to "Finishing Techniques" on pages 9–12 for detailed instructions.

1. Layer the quilt top, batting, and backing; baste the layers together.

2. Free-motion outline quilt around the vine and leaves in the center section. Quilt a large design in the area surrounded by the vine. Stipple quilt the background outside the vine.

3. Quilt in the ditch on both sides of the inner border. Add a zigzag pattern to the inner border.

4. On the outer border, outline quilt around the vine and leaves and stipple quilt the background.

5. Bind the quilt using the 3"-wide binding strips.

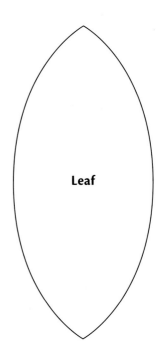

Leaf

RASPBERRY KISS

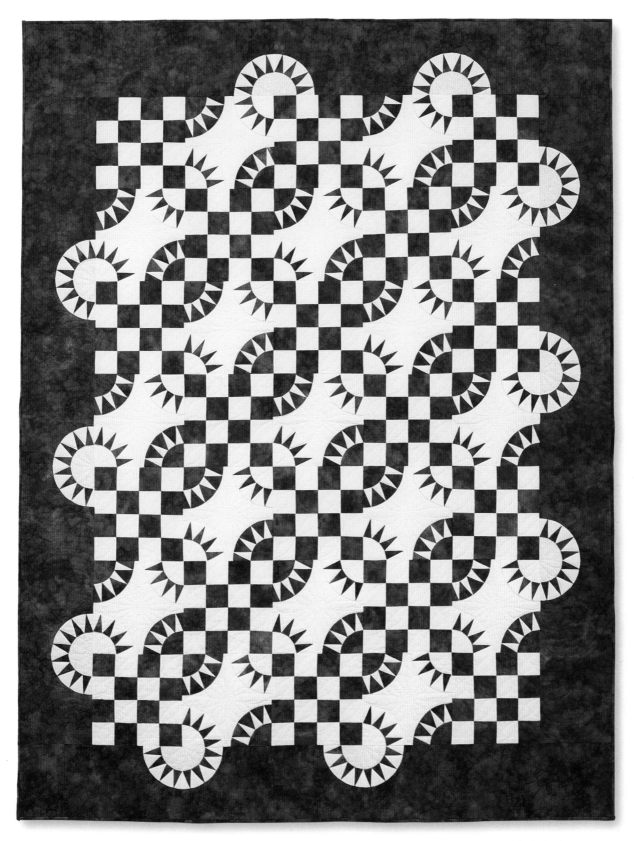

Finished Quilt: 66½" x 86½" • **Finished Block: 10" x 10"**

Raspberry Kiss

Fill a mixing glass with ice.

1 oz black raspberry liqueur

1 oz dark crème de cacao

1 oz milk or cream

Shake.

Strain into chilled glass.

Even though this raspberry patch is filled with prickly thorns, working them into your design is painless when you use paper-piecing techniques to create the sharp points of the appliquéd arcs. Extended into the border, the complex-looking arcs make this simple two-color quilt appear much more complicated than it really is.

MATERIALS

Yardages are based on 42"-wide fabrics.

6⅓ yards of dark fabric for blocks, border, and binding

5⅝ yards of light fabric for blocks

5½ yards of fabric for backing

70" x 90" piece of batting

2 yards of 45"-wide lightweight nonfusible interfacing

CUTTING

All measurements include ¼"-wide seam allowances. Cut all strips across the width of the fabric.

From the dark fabric, cut:

36 strips, 3" x 42". Set aside 33 strips; crosscut the remaining 3 strips into 34 squares, 3" x 3".

8 strips, 8½" x 42"

8 binding strips, 3" x 42"

From the light fabric, cut:

39 strips, 3" x 42". Set aside 37 strips; crosscut the remaining 2 strips into 10 rectangles, 3" x 6½".

6 strips, 10½" x 42"; crosscut into 17 squares, 10½" x 10½".

From the interfacing, cut:

8 strips, 7¾" x 45"

MAKING THE 16 PATCH BLOCKS

1. Sew two light and two dark 3" x 42" strips together along the long edges as shown. Make six strip sets. Press the seam allowances toward the dark strips. Crosscut the strip sets into 72 segments, 3" wide.

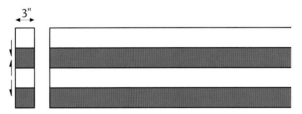

Make 6 strip sets.
Cut 72 segments.

2. Sew four segments together, alternating the direction of each segment as shown to make the block. Repeat to make a total of 18 blocks.

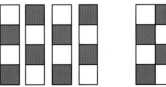

Make 18.

Making the Appliquéd Blocks

1. Make 88 copies of the arc pattern on page 61.

2. Referring to "Paper Piecing" on page 7, use the 3" x 42" light and dark strips to make 34 appliqués with dark backgrounds (odd-numbered areas) and light spikes (even-numbered areas), and 54 appliqués with light backgrounds and dark spikes.

Make 34.   Make 54.

3. Set aside 20 appliqués with light backgrounds for the border. With the *paper side up*, pin the remaining appliqués to six of the interfacing strips. You will cut inside the pattern lines when you cut out the shapes, so you do not need to leave much space between shapes. Sew on the pattern sewing lines along the top and bottom curved edges, leaving the ends open. Backstitch at the beginning and end of each seam.

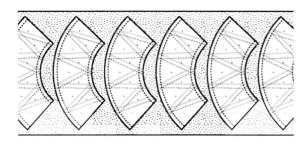

4. Cut out each appliqué, cutting through the paper, interfacing, and fabric just inside the solid lines along the top and bottom of the arcs, leaving ⅛" to ¼" for seam allowance. For the ends of the arcs, measure and cut through all layers, leaving *exactly* ¼" for seam allowance.

5. Remove the paper from the bottom curved seam allowance only and clip the inner curve of each appliqué.

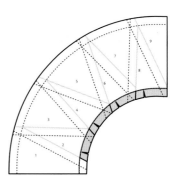

6. Remove the remainder of the paper from each appliqué.

7. Turn the appliqués right side out. Smooth out the curves and finger-press the fabric slightly over the interfacing side so that the interfacing won't show on the finished quilt. Use an iron to press each arc from the fabric side.

8. With right sides up, place a dark 3" square in opposite corners of each light 10½" square, aligning the raw edges.

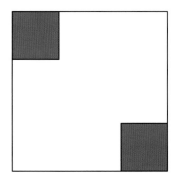

9. Place an appliqué with a dark background over the corners with the dark squares, and an appliqué with a light background in the remaining two corners, aligning the straight edges of the appliqués with the background squares. Pin the pieces in place. Appliqué the arcs in place along the curved edges, using a blanket stitch, blind hem stitch, or narrow

Assembling the Quilt Top

1. Lay out the blocks in seven rows, alternating the blocks in each row and from row to row. Be sure the blocks are positioned with the dark fabric in the upper-left and lower-right corners. Sew the blocks in each row together. Press the seam allowances toward the 16 Patch blocks. Sew the rows together. Press the seam allowances in one direction.

zigzag stitch. On the back of each block, trim away the light fabric under each appliqué and dark square, leaving ⅛" to ¼" for seam allowance.

Make 17.

2. Sew the paper-pieced appliqués with light backgrounds that you set aside earlier into pairs to form 10 half circles. Pin the half circles to the remaining two interfacing strips. Sew on the pattern sewing lines along the top and bottom curved edges, backstitching at the beginning and end of each seam. Repeat steps 4–7 of "Making the Appliquéd Blocks" to finish making the appliqués.

3. With right sides up, lay each half circle over a light rectangle so that the open area along the bottom of each half circle is filled. Appliqué the half circles to the rectangles along the inner curve. Trim away the excess rectangle fabric, leaving ⅛" to ¼" for seam allowance.

4. Refer to the photo on page 55 to position the half circles along the edges of the quilt. Once you have determined the location, place the half circle on the quilt top, right sides together and straight edges aligned. The seam of each half circle should align with the seam joining the appliquéd block and the 16 Patch block. Pin the half circles in place.

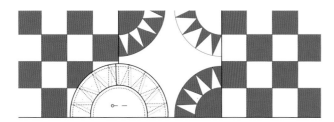

5. Refer to "Adding Borders" on page 9 to add the borders to the quilt top, piecing the strips as needed to achieve the exact length. You will be securing the half circles in the seam as the borders are added.

6. Press the half circles toward the borders. Appliqué each half circle in place along the outer curved edge.

FINISHING THE QUILT

Refer to "Finishing Techniques" on pages 9–12 for detailed instructions.

1. Layer the quilt top, batting, and backing; baste the layers together.

2. Quilt in the ditch between all the blocks and between the blocks and border to stabilize the quilt.

3. Drop the feed dogs and free-motion quilt in the ditch along the inner and outer curve of each arc and around each point.

4. Quilt the designs shown in the remaining areas of the blocks.

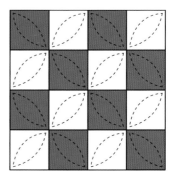

5. Quilt in the ditch along the inner and outer curve of each border half circle and around each point. Quilt a border design in the remaining area of the border.

6. Bind the quilt with the dark 3"-wide strips.

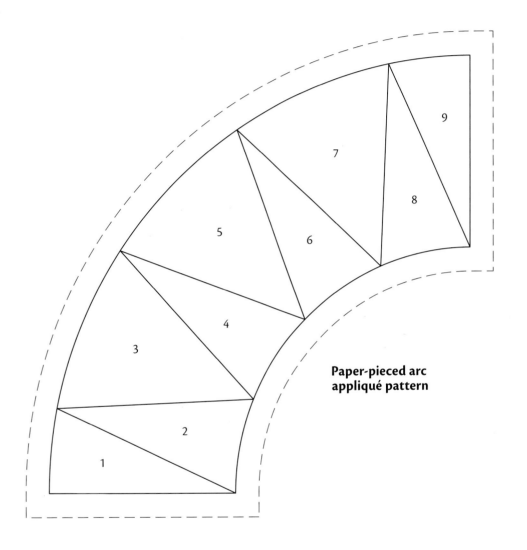

Paper-pieced arc appliqué pattern

BLUE CANARY

Finished Quilt: 46½" x 46½" • Finished Block: 8½" x 8½"

Making a two-color quilt doesn't mean you have to limit yourself to just two fabrics. Case in point: this zippy wall hanging that uses multiple blue and gold prints for the block backgrounds as well as for the paper-pieced appliqués that create a wave of excitement.

MATERIALS

Yardages are based on 42"-wide fabrics.

2¾ yards *total* of assorted gold prints for blocks

2¾ yards *total* of assorted blue prints for blocks

2 yards of dark blue print for border and binding

3 yards of fabric for backing

50" x 50" piece of batting

1½ yards of 45"-wide lightweight nonfusible interfacing

CUTTING

All measurements include ¼"-wide seam allowances. Cut all strips across the width of the fabric unless otherwise indicated.

From the assorted gold prints, cut a *total* of:
8 squares, 9" x 9"
26 strips, 2½" x 42"

From the assorted blue prints, cut a *total* of:
8 squares, 9" x 9"
26 strips, 2½" x 42"

From the interfacing, cut:
6 strips, 8" x 45"

From the *lengthwise* grain of the dark blue print for border, cut:
4 strips, 4" x 34½"
4 strips, 4" x 48½"

From the remainder of the dark blue print, cut:
5 binding strips, 3" x 42"

MAKING THE BLOCKS

1. Make 26 copies of the appliqué pattern on page 67.

2. Refer to "Paper Piecing" on page 7 to paper piece each appliqué shape, using one gold and one blue 2½" x 42" strip for each appliqué. Use the blue strips for the even-numbered areas and the gold strips for the odd-numbered areas.

Make 26.

Blue Canary

Fill a serving glass with ice.
1½ oz gin
½ oz blue curaçao
Fill with grapefruit juice.
Shake.

3. With the *paper side up*, pin the paper-pieced shapes to the interfacing strips. You will cut inside the pattern lines when you cut out the shapes, so you do not need to leave much space between shapes. Sew on the pattern sewing lines around each shape, slightly overlapping the stitching at the beginning and end of each seam.

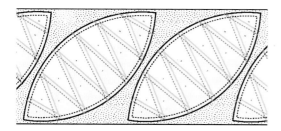

4. Cut out each shape, cutting through the paper, interfacing, and fabric just inside the solid lines, leaving ⅛" to ¼" for seam allowance. Cut a slit in the interfacing of each shape.

5. Remove all the paper. Using a turning tool, turn the shape right side out, smoothing out the curves and pushing out the points. Finger-press the fabric slightly over the interfacing side so that the interfacing won't show on the finished quilt. Use an iron to press each shape from the fabric side.

6. With right sides up, center and pin a paper-pieced appliqué shape diagonally on each 9" square. Appliqué the shapes in place, using a blanket stitch, blind hem stitch, or narrow zigzag stitch to complete the blocks. If desired, trim away the fabric and interfacing under each appliqué shape, leaving ⅛" to ¼"

for seam allowance. Set aside the remaining 10 appliqué shapes for the border.

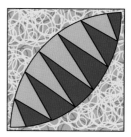

ASSEMBLING THE QUILT TOP

1. Arrange the blocks in four rows of four blocks each as shown, alternating the gold and blue backgrounds in each row and from row to row. Rotate the blocks so that the appliqué points meet and form four circles. The gold spikes should point toward the inside of the circle and the blue spikes should point toward the outside of the circle.

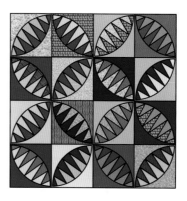

2. Cut the remaining 10 appliqué shapes in half from point to point. One half of each shape will have gold points on a blue background and the other half will have blue points on a gold background.

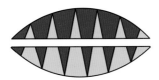

3. Mark the crosswise center of each dark blue 4" x 34½" strip. Lay two strips together along the long edges, matching centers. Center and pin three halved appliqué shapes with gold points onto one border strip and two halves with blue points onto the other border strip as shown. Appliqué the shapes in place. From the wrong side of the border, trim away the fabric and interfacing behind each appliqué, leaving ⅛" to ¼" for seam allowance and being careful not to cut into the border fabric. Repeat with the remaining two strips. Sew these borders to the sides of the quilt center.

Center

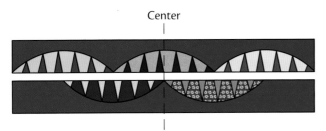

Sew border strips together.

4. Repeat step 3 with the remaining appliqué halves and the dark blue 4" x 48½" strips, reversing the color placement. Sew these borders to the top and bottom edges of the quilt center.

FINISHING THE QUILT

Refer to "Finishing Techniques" on pages 9–12 for detailed instructions.

1. Layer the quilt top, batting, and backing; baste the layers together.

2. For the blocks, quilt in the ditch around the blocks, the appliqués, and the points of each appliqué. Crosshatch a 1" grid in the background of each block.

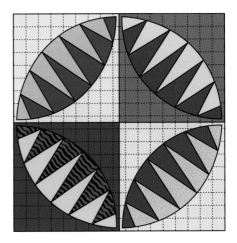

3. On the border, quilt in the ditch around the appliqués and the appliqué points. Drop the feed dogs and free-motion quilt a zigzag pattern in the background, except for the corners. In the corners, quilt parallel lines at right angles, ½" apart.

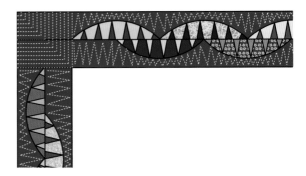

4. Bind the quilt using the dark blue 3"-wide strips.

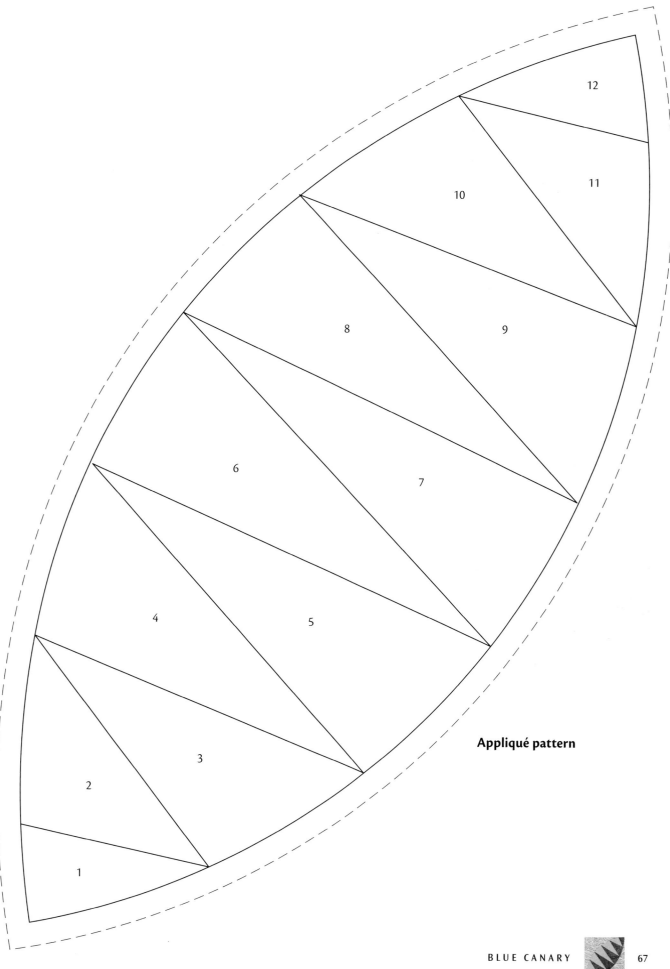

Appliqué pattern

SUNSET ISLAND

Finished Quilt: 83" x 105½" • **Finished Drunkard's Path Variation Block:** 22½" x 22½" • **Finished Border Block:** 7½" x 7½"

Call on your stash of plaid fabrics and a sunny yellow background print to give this Drunkard's Path variation a fresh new look. You'll feel like you're soaking up the sun on your own private island every time you wrap up in it.

MATERIALS

Yardages are based on 42"-wide fabrics.

9 yards of yellow print for blocks and binding

7⅓ yards *total* of assorted plaid prints for blocks*

5⅓ yards of 45"-wide lightweight nonfusible interfacing

7¼ yards of fabric for backing

86" x 109" piece of batting

Template plastic

Scraps can be used for some pieces but they need to be no smaller than 6½" square. You will also need several 8½"-wide full-width strips. Refer to the cut-ting instructions for specifics.

CUTTING

All measurements include ¼"-wide seam allowances. Cut all strips across the width of the fabric unless otherwise indicated.

From the interfacing, cut:

27 strips, 6½" x 45"

From the yellow print, cut:

22 strips, 8½" x 42"; crosscut into 87 squares,
 8½" x 8½"

12 strips, 6½" x 42"

10 binding strips, 3" x 42"

From the assorted plaid prints, cut a *total* of:

17 strips, 8½" x 42"; crosscut into 67 squares,
 8½" x 8½"

87 squares, 6½" x 6½"

MAKING THE DRUNKARD'S PATH BLOCKS

1. Make a plastic template of the circle pattern on page 73.

2. Using the template, trace 154 circles onto the interfacing strips. Leave approximately ½" of space between shapes. You should be able to fit six circles per strip. Cut apart 87 circles, leaving at least a ¼" margin of interfacing. Leave the remaining circles joined in strips.

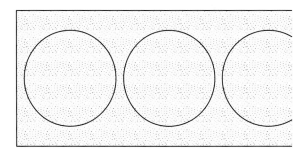

3. With right sides up, pin a marked interfacing strip to each yellow 6½" x 42" strip. Pin an individual interfacing circle to each plaid 6½" square. Sew on the marked lines, overlapping the stitching at the beginning and end of each seam.

Sunset Island (nonalcoholic)

4 oz pineapple juice

1 oz coconut cream

½ cup crushed ice

In a blender, combine all ingredients.

Blend well.

Pour into a Collins glass.

4. Cut out the circles, leaving ⅛" to ¼" for seam allowance. Cut a slit in the interfacing and turn the circles right side out. Smooth out the curves and finger-press the fabric slightly over the interfacing side so that the interfacing won't show on the finished quilt. Use an iron to press each circle from the fabric side.

5. Fold each of the yellow and the plaid 8½" squares in half and finger-press along the center of the fold. Fold the squares in half in the opposite direction and finger-press the fold again. When you open up the square there should be an X marking the center.

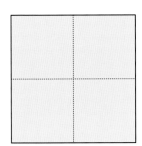

6. Repeat step 5 with each of the yellow and the plaid appliqués to mark the centers.

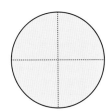

7. With right sides up, insert a pin through the center of a plaid circle and then through the center of a yellow square. Rotate the circle so the straight of grain of the circle matches the straight of grain of the square. Pin the appliqué to the square. Repeat with the remaining plaid circles and yellow squares.

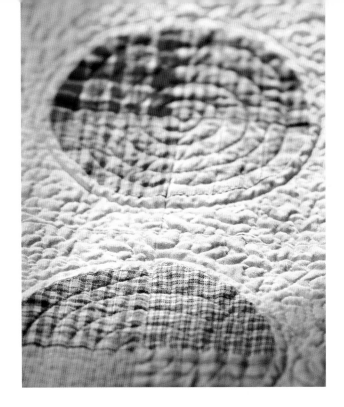

8. Repeat step 7 with the plaid squares and yellow circles.

9. Appliqué the circles to the squares, using a blanket stitch, blind hem stitch, or narrow zigzag stitch.

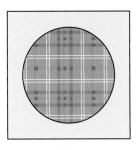
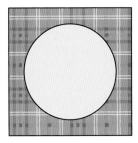

Make 87.   Make 67.

10. Cut each square into quarters. The appliqué process can draw up the background fabric, so measure the square from each side to find the center. Keep pieces with plaid backgrounds separate from pieces with yellow backgrounds.

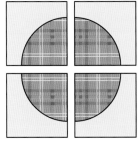

11. On the back of each quarter, trim away the fabric and interfacing under each quartered circle portion, leaving ⅛" to ¼" for seam allowance.

12. Lay out the quartered pieces in six rows of six pieces each as shown. Use a variety of plaid fabrics and be careful that the background color is correct for each piece. Sew the pieces in each row together. Press the seam allowances in opposite directions from row to row. Sew the rows together. Press the seam allowances in one direction. Repeat to make a total of 12 blocks. Set aside the remaining quartered pieces for the border blocks.

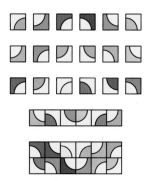

Make 12.

ASSEMBLING THE QUILT TOP

1. Lay out the blocks in four rows of three blocks each. Rotate the blocks so that the seam allowances of the blocks in each row will abut when joined. Sew the blocks in each row together. Press the seam allowances in opposite directions from row to row. Sew the rows together. Press the seam allowances in one direction.

2. To make the border blocks, sew the remaining quartered pieces together as shown to make 32 Circle blocks and 14 alternate blocks.

Make 32.   Make 14.

3. Refer to the assembly diagram below to sew eight Circle blocks and four alternate blocks together side by side as shown for the side borders. Make two. Join the borders to the sides of the quilt center. Press the seam allowances toward the borders.

4. Refer to the assembly diagram to sew eight Circle blocks and three alternate blocks together side by side as shown for the top and bottom borders. Make two. Join the borders to the top and bottom of the quilt center. Press the seam allowances toward the borders.

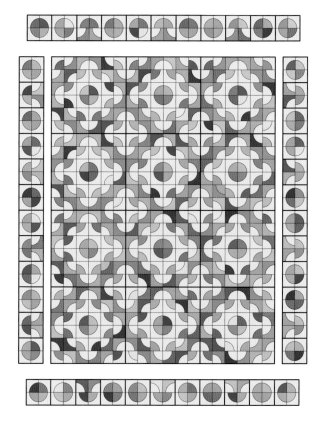

FINISHING THE QUILT

Refer to "Finishing Techniques" on pages 9–12 for detailed instructions.

1. Layer the quilt top, batting, and backing; baste the layers together.

2. Drop the feed dogs and free-motion outline quilt around the plaid areas, including the plaid circles in the blocks and borders.

3. On each plaid circle, quilt a concentric circle that begins at the outside of the circle and ends at the center of the circle.

4. Stipple quilt in all the yellow areas. Echo quilt in the remaining plaid areas.

5. Bind the quilt with the yellow 3"-wide strips.

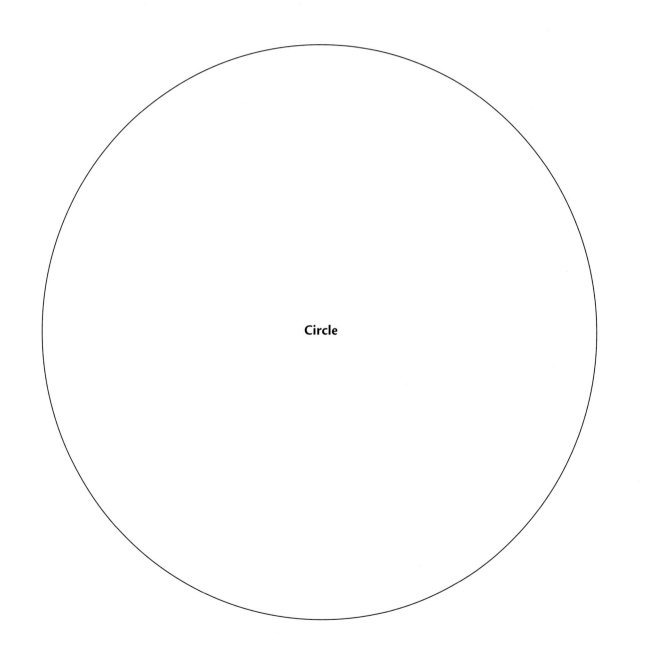

Circle

Finished Quilt: 42¼" x 42¼" • **Finished Block:** 8" x 8"

As delightfully refreshing as the drink after which it is named, this small quilt is sure to be the focal point of any room. The illusion of circles is created by framing the appliquéd flower blocks with the curves of the alternate blocks and setting them on point.

MATERIALS

Yardages are based on 42″-wide fabrics.

1½ yards of cream print 1 for background

1⅛ yards of pink print 1 for border and binding

⅔ yard of green print for arc and flower center appliqués

⅝ yard of pink print 2 for outer petal appliqués

¼ yard of cream print 2 for inner petal appliqués

1½ yards of fabric for backing

46" x 46" piece of batting

1½ yards of 45"-wide lightweight nonfusible interfacing

Template plastic

Water-soluble marker

CUTTING

All measurements include ¼″-wide seam allowances. Cut all strips across the width of the fabric.

From the interfacing, cut:

4 strips, 4¼" x 45"

2 strips, 3¾" x 45"

1 strip, 2¼" x 45"

6 strips, 3" x 45"

From pink print 2, cut:

4 strips, 4¼" x 42"

From cream print 2, cut:

2 strips, 3¾" x 42"

From the green print, cut:

6 strips, 3" x 42"

1 strip, 2¼" x 42"

From cream print 1, cut:

4 strips, 8½" x 42"; crosscut into 13 squares, 8½" x 8½"

2 squares, 12½" x 12½"; cut each square in half diagonally twice to yield 8 side setting triangles

2 squares, 6½" x 6½"; cut each square in half diagonally to yield 4 corner setting triangles

From pink print 1, cut:

4 strips, 4½" x 42"

5 binding strips, 3" x 42"

MAKING THE APPLIQUÉD BLOCKS

1. Make a plastic template for the outer petal, inner petal, and flower center appliqué shapes, using the patterns on page 79.

2. Using the outer petal template, trace 36 shapes onto the 4¼" x 45" interfacing strips. Use the inner petal template to trace 36 shapes onto the 3¾" x 45" interfacing strips. On the 2¼" x 45" interfacing strip, use the flower center template to trace nine shapes.

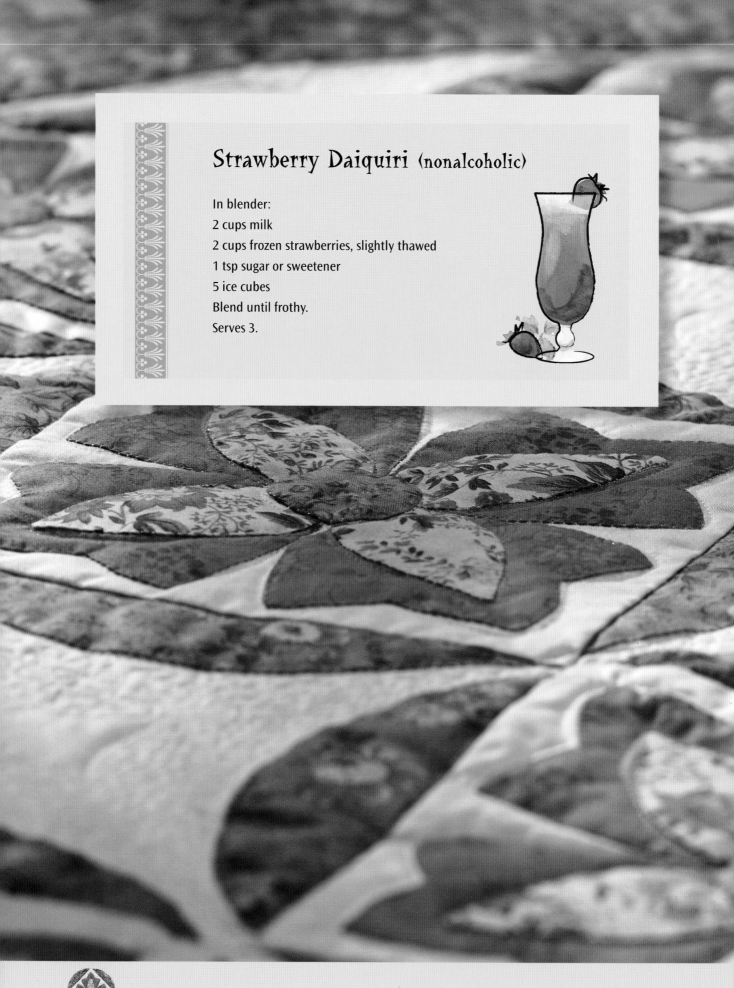

Strawberry Daiquiri (nonalcoholic)

In blender:

2 cups milk

2 cups frozen strawberries, slightly thawed

1 tsp sugar or sweetener

5 ice cubes

Blend until frothy.

Serves 3.

Leave approximately ½" of space between shapes. *Do not* cut out the shapes.

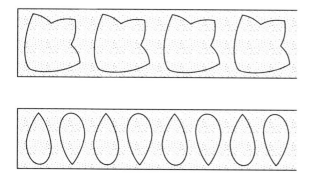

3. With right sides up, pin each outer petal interfacing strip to a pink print 2 strip, and each inner petal interfacing strip to a cream print strip. Pin the flower center interfacing strip to the green print 2¼" x 42" strip. Sew on the marked lines of each shape, slightly overlapping the stitching at the beginning and end of each seam.

4. Cut out the appliqué shapes, leaving ⅛" to ¼" for seam allowance. Clip the inner points of the outer petal shapes. Cut a slit in the interfacing of each shape and turn the appliqués right side out. Use a turning tool to smooth the curves and push out the points. Finger-press the fabric slightly over the interfacing side so that the interfacing won't show on the finished quilt. Use an iron to press each shape from the fabric side.

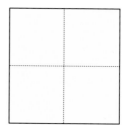

5. Position an inner petal appliqué on each outer petal appliqué as shown and appliqué it in place, using a blanket stitch, blind hem stitch, or narrow zigzag stitch. If desired, trim the fabric behind the inner petal appliqué, leaving ⅛" to ¼" for seam allowance.

6. Fold nine cream print 1 squares in half and finger-press the fold. Open up the squares and fold them in half in the opposite direction; finger-press the folds.

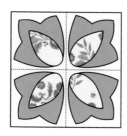

7. Position an appliquéd flower unit from step 5 in each quadrant of each square from step 6 so that the sides almost touch. Pin the appliqués in place. Pin a flower center appliqué in the center of each square. Appliqué the shapes in place. Make nine blocks.

Make 9.

MAKING THE ALTERNATE BLOCKS

1. Make a plastic template for the arc appliqué, using the pattern on page 79.

2. Using the template, trace 36 shapes onto the 3" x 45" interfacing strips, aligning the template straight edge with the interfacing long edges and tracing shapes along both sides of the strip as shown. Leave approximately ½" of space between shapes. You should be able to fit approximately seven shapes per strip. *Do not* cut out the shapes.

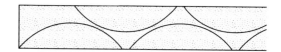

3. With right sides up, pin a marked interfacing strip to each green print 3" x 42" strip. Sew on the marked lines, backstitching at the beginning and end of each seam.

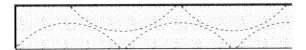

4. Cut out the appliqué shapes, leaving ⅛" to ¼" for seam allowance. Turn the appliqués right side out, smoothing out the curves and finger-pressing the fabric slightly over the interfacing side so that the interfacing won't show on the finished quilt. Use an iron to press each shape from the fabric side.

5. Center and pin an appliqué to each side of the remaining four cream print 1 squares. Appliqué the curved edge of each shape in place, using a blanket stitch, blind hem stitch, or narrow zigzag stitch. Set aside the remaining appliqués for the setting triangles.

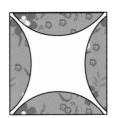

Make 4.

6. From the wrong side of the blocks, trim away the fabric and interfacing behind each appliqué, leaving ⅛" to ¼" for seam allowance and being careful not to cut into the top fabric.

Assembling the Quilt Top

1. Using the arc appliqués you set aside earlier, center an appliqué on the short sides of each cream print 1 side setting triangle and on the long side of each cream print 1 corner setting triangle. Appliqué them in place.

Make 8.   Make 4.

2. Lay out the blocks and setting triangles in diagonal rows as shown, alternating the appliquéd blocks and alternate blocks in each row and from row to row. Sew the blocks and setting triangles in each row together. Press the seam allowances toward the appliquéd blocks. Sew the rows together. Press the seam allowances toward the center row. Add the remaining corner setting triangles. Press the seam allowances toward the center row.

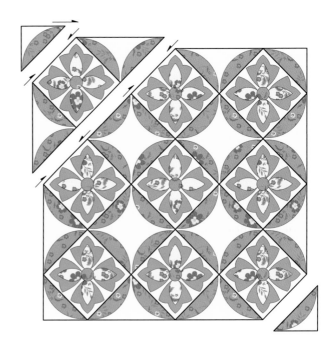

3. Refer to "Adding Borders" on page 9 to sew the 4½"-wide border strips of pink print 1 to the quilt center.

Finishing the Quilt

Refer to "Finishing Techniques" on pages 9–12 for detailed instructions.

1. Layer the quilt top, batting, and backing; baste the layers together.

2. Quilt in the ditch between all the blocks and along the border seam to stabilize the quilt.

3. Drop the feed dogs and free-motion quilt along the curved edges of the arc appliqués.

4. On the appliquéd blocks, outline quilt around each outer petal, inner petal, and flower center shape.

5. Using a water-soluble marker, trace the quilting pattern below right onto the center of each alternate block. Quilt on the traced lines and then fill in the area outside the design with stipple quilting.

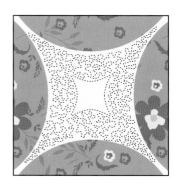

6. I quilted the border with a repeating series of two arc shapes nested together, similar to the design shown on page 23.

7. Bind the quilt with the 3"-wide pink strips.

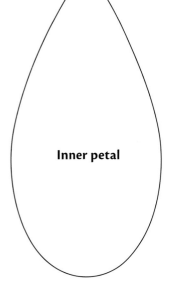

Inner petal

Flower center

Arc

Outer petal

Quilting pattern

About the Author

As a small child, Lori Buhler learned many forms of needlework, including sewing, from her mother. She began her endeavor into quilting in the 1980s and hasn't looked back since. Although she began making quilts using traditional hand-sewing methods, she has learned to appreciate the faster results of machine work. In addition to being an active member of several quilting groups, she has also won numerous regional awards, including Quilter of the Year from the Cal-Co Quilters' Guild in 2001. Lori enjoys all aspects of quilt-making, but especially likes finding easier ways to achieve a more complicated look for today's busy quilters.

Lori resides in Battle Creek, Michigan, with her husband, Dave; daughter, Amanda; a big brown dog named Zeke; and a little gray cat named Zoey.